I0150298

The Mass and its Folklore

John Hobson Matthews

Catholic Authors Press
2007

First published 1903
Copyright 2007 Catholic Authors Press

ISBN: 978-0-9783198-2-3

Catholic Authors Press

Hartford, Connecticut

www.CatholicAuthors.org

PREFACE

꙱

THERE are many good and popular English
books on the Mass. Some of them treat the
subject after the manner of a *Rationale*, ex-
plaining the significance of the prayers and
ceremonies of the Eucharistic rite; others
are historical and antiquarian, and eluci-
date the origin and evolution of the ceremonial—while of devotional works there is
no end. It appeared, however, that there
was room for a short treatise on the folklore
and minor antiquities of the Mass; by which
are meant the various aspects and the numerous details of the Holy Sacrifice which
have so impressed the minds of Catholics in
the past as to leave permanent traces in the
popular traditions and speech. The aim
of this little book is to stimulate love for the
Mass by showing how it was valued by our
ancestors in the ages of faith, and what our

predecessors in the penal times willingly suffered for its sake.

The Church, being the Catholic Church, has many ways of leading her children along the pathway to heaven. Her chief effort, the primary object of her existence, is to secure the salvation of all men by every means in her power. And since the collective human mind comprises an infinite variety in intellect, character, temperament, imagination and taste, the Church (making herself "all things to all men") adapts with like diversity the forces which she brings to bear upon mankind, including her ritual, her discipline and her methods of worship both public and private.

At the same time, there can be no doubt that the spirit of antiquity strongly permeates the services of the Catholic Church—the most conservative institution on earth, as well as the most democratic—and that those are entirely in harmony with the genius of Catholicism who are animated with a profound reverence for the pomp and solemnity of the Church's public offices, and with a tender love for even the most homely religious traditions and practices of our Catholic forefathers.

While some ot us may be more attracted by the Church's conservatism and others by her vigorous modernity, we are all bound to respect equally Catholic antiquity and papal sanction. Both these authorities are of the highest kind—are, in fact, identical. Rome permits no deviation from the Catholic standard in her devotions, and the freshest flowers in her "garden of the soul" have their roots deep down in the rich soil of the Church's past.

Cardiff, Feast of St David, 1903.

CONTENTS

The Mass and its Folklore

❧

I--Introductory

THE Mass is the liturgical rite whereby the Catholic Church, from the Last Supper until this very morning, has celebrated throughout the world the divine mystery of the Passion and Death of our Lord Jesus Christ. It is His perpetuation of the one sacrifice of the Cross. It is the great act of worship of historic Christianity, the mainspring of the Church's mechanism, the throbbing heart of the Bride of Christ. Whether celebrated by mitred prelate amid the clustered columns and tinted lights of some Gothic cathedral, with all the splendid accessories of ecclesiastical pomp, or by a poor blackrobe missionary in a wigwam of the Far West, the Mass is the supreme and central Catholic worship; the one great reality, as Carlyle deemed it, which yet survives in an age of unsubstantial insincerities. As a still more modern thinker* has pithily said, "It is the Mass that matters." It was for the Mass that the ancient Briton constructed his wattled *eglwys*, the Gael his drystone oratory. For this the Norman baron built the parish church hard by his manor-house, and the lord abbot erected his stately minster. For the sake of the Mass the painter, the goldsmith, the scribe and the limner, produced the masterpieces of art which are the despair of our artistically degenerate age.

Though we know but little of the precise mode in which the sacred mysteries were solemnized by the apostles themselves, there is abundant evidence in the writings of the early fathers that in the sub-apostolic age the necessity for the decent and orderly celebration of the Eucharist had led to the formation of a liturgy with a definite ritual. When once the infant Church had emerged from the catacombs into the enjoyment of political freedom, this primitive ritual rapidly

* Mr Augustine Birrell.

developed in ornateness and, hallowed by time, was lovingly enshrined in a rich outer casket of popular sentiment and tradition, studded with gems of poetry and folklore.

The word "Mass" is in Latin *missa*, Italian *messa*, Spanish *misa*, French *messe*, Saxon *mæsse*, German *messe*. It is thought to be connected with the words *Ite, missa est,* pronounced by the priest at the conclusion of the rite; and the editors of the "Catholic Dictionary" adduce some evidence to support this derivation. Although the word is, in nearly all the languages of the Western Church, derived from the Latin *missa*, this is not universally the case. Thus the Celtic tongues name it by a word of purely native origin, namely, Irish *aiffrionn*, Welsh *offeren;* and in Maltese it is expressed by the Arabic word *koddiesa*—" the sacred thing."

The Mass has left upon the English language marks which centuries of Protestantism have not been able to efface. Our greatest festival is still called "Christmas," i.e., "the Christ Mass." An attempt was made, in the age of Puritan ascendancy, not only to abolish Christmas, but also to eradicate its name by substituting the term " Christ-tide"; but ancient custom proved too strong for the innovators, and the Mass conquered once more. We have also Candlemas, Lammas, Martinmas, Michaelmas, Childermas and other words of similar formation—which is one almost peculiar to the English tongue. The earliest Mass in our old churches was called the Morrow-Mass. There were also the Jesus Mass and the Lady Mass. In the same manner were formed the old English words " mass-priest" and " mass-penny." In a later age the Protestants dubbed our poor chapels " mass-houses "; and we still sometimes call a missal a " mass-book."

In French there are several proverbial phrases bearing reference to the Mass. Thus, of a man who eats a big breakfast before attending early Mass, they say : " He is going to the Mass of the Dead, he takes bread and wine with him." " Going to Midnight Mass" is an ironical term applied to a person who haunts taverns late at night.

A hypocrite is sometimes spoken of as "a man who hears two Masses." Of another they will say: " He has made a short Mass, he will make a long dinner." " He goes neither to Mass nor sermon," is said of an irreligious person.

Mass is celebrated only during the first half of the day, the twelve hours from midnight to noon. Most frequently Mass is said in the early morn.* It is peculiarly a morning service. To this rule there are hardly any exceptions. There is a church at Naples which from time immemorial has possessed the peculiar privilege of a Mass said at two o'clock after noon. A Mass may be commenced at noon, in which case it will end between half an hour and an hour after; or it may, on rare occasions, be begun before midnight, provided the consecration does not take place before the stroke of twelve.

A priest may only say one Mass a day. But on Christmas Day he says three Masses,

---

* " Best refection, to gladden all our cheer,
  Is every morrow early to hear a Mass."
                                    —LYDGATE.

in honour of the solemn mystery of the
Incarnation. Of these three, the first is—in
theory, though not always in practice—to be
said or sung at midnight of Christmas Eve,
the second at daybreak and the third in the
forenoon. Commonly, however, a priest says
three low Masses in quick succession on
Christmas morning early.

At St John's Church, Valetta, Malta, a
low Mass is said on every holiday of obligation at 12 noon. It is called *La Messa dei
pigri*—" The lazy folk's Mass," testifying to
the fact that the Mass is essentially a morning act of worship. I once heard an excel-
lent but generally prejudiced Nonconformist
say : " One thing I do admire in Roman
Catholicism : it is a six-o'clock-in-the-morning
religion," which he evidently considered as
admirable a thing as " two-o'clock-in-the-
morning courage."

The celebrant always says Mass abso-
lutely fasting : i.e., he must not have tasted
food or drink from the previous midnight.
This rule has been framed out of reverence
for the Eucharist. A legend is current in

Malta that one day, towards the end of the eighteenth century, when the Knights of Saint John were to make their Easter Communion together in their conventual church, a young knight expressed his intention of taking a meal after midnight. When remonstrated with upon this sacrilegious resolve, he defended himself by saying that it was moie respectful to receive the Host upon food, than to put food upon the Host. The story goes no further, being considered by the Maltese, in this inconclusive form, a sufficient object-lesson in impiety.

One of the most ancient and indispensable rules requires that Mass should be celebrated upon an altar of stone ; but, although the whole structure of the altar must in general be stone, the law is, in certain cases, held to be observed when the lower portion is of wood, provided the altar-stone be of the required material. The altar-stone, before it can be used, must be consecrated by the bishop according to the form laid down in the *Pontificale Romanum.* Five small equilinear crosses are incised upon its surface, one at each corner and one in the middle, and a small square cavity is made near one side.   At the consecration of the altar-stone the crosses are anointed with chrism, and relics are deposited in the cavity, which is thereupon sealed up.   Portable altar-stones are sometimes consecrated for the use of itinerant clergy, such as missionaries in remote and uncivilized countries, where no churches are to be found.

The priest celebrates Mass standing with his back to the congregation.   At St Peter's and the other basilicas in Rome, however, the Pope celebrates Mass on the opposite side of the altar, which stands insulated, and thus faces the congregation.

A High Mass is one which is accompanied with the full ceremonial.   In Latin it is termed *Missa Solemnis*.

Mass which is performed by the celebrant alone, without deacon or sub-deacon, and assisted by a simple clerk or server, but chanted, and with or without incense and the six lights, is termed *Missa Cantata*, "Sung Mass."   Of this kind is the last or parochial

Mass in our small mission churches. It is often, but erroneously, called " High Mass." At such a Mass the clerk or server must wear cassock and surplice or cotta, and there are often several acolytes to assist.

Low Mass is said by the priest without chant or incense, with a simple clerk or server, who need not wear cassock, surplice or cotta. There are only two lights on the altar.

Every Catholic of the age of seven years and upwards is bound, under pain of mortal sin, to attend Mass on all Sundays and " holidays of obligation," unless prevented by sickness, remoteness, or other lawful and *bonâ-fide* excuse. A Catholic may not, without some good reason, take up his abode in a place where he knows or suspects that he will not be able to get Mass. Also, he is in conscience bound to see that all Catholics over whom he has any authority, parental or other, perform their duty in this respect.

Mass is the only public service which the Church obliges her children to take part in. Vespers, Compline and Benediction are also solemn and beautiful liturgical functions ; the

service of Good Friday morning is largely
made up of the prayers and manual acts of
the Mass.   Yet the Church, desirous as she
is that we should benefit by participation in
these devout services, does not bind us to
attend them under pain of mortal sin.   That
supreme sanction is reserved to the Mass
alone; and even the Good Friday service
(" Mass of the Presanctified " * as it is
called), because it comes short of being the
Holy Sacrifice, is not " of obligation."   It is
the Mass that matters.

The question is often asked by Catholics :
How much of the Mass must be heard in
order to " fulfil the precept " ?   The Church
has not seen fit to state definitely what is the
irreducible minimum ; but it is generally
held and seems certain that it is essential to
be present before the commencement of the
Offertory, and to remain until after the
priest's Communion.

* The Host has been consecrated on the previous day ; hence this service is no true Mass.
Consecration, as well as Communion, is essential
to the Sacrifice.

II.-The Virtue of the Mass

Much as devout Catholics of the present
day revere the Holy Sacrifice and the Blessed
Sacrament of the Altar, it is only with diffi-
culty that we can form an adequate notion of
the profound and enthusiastic devotion felt
towards the Mass by the people of this
country in the ages of faith.   One is amazed,
in reading ancient manuscripts, at the raptu-
rous sentiments and language of their writers
on this subject.   To say that the Mass was
the centre and heart of our ancestors' religion is to employ an inadequate phrase ; it
was their very life and breath.   It is to
the point to mention that the commonest
oath in England was "by the Mass"—for
people swear by what they regard as most
sacred.

No one who has read the old Welsh and
English tales on which Tennyson founded
his Arthurian idylls, can have failed to be
struck with their frequent allusions to the

Mass. King Arthur's knights, good, bad and indifferent, all turn in to wayside chapels to hear Mass, as naturally as in the present day their descendants would enter the news-rooms of their various clubs. It would seem, too, that the hearing of Mass always preceded the taking of the morning meal: "And on the morrow he heard Mass, and brake his fast," is one of the commonplaces of the chronicles of the Round Table. "And Sir Launcelot awoke, and went and took his horse, and rode all day and all that night in a forest; and at the last he was aware of a hermitage, and a chapel that stood between two cliffs. And then he heard a little bell ring to Mass; and thither he rode, and alighted, and tied his horse to the gate, and heard Mass. And he that sang the Mass was the Bishop of Canterbury."

Dan John Lydgate, a Benedictine monk and the contemporary of Chaucer, wrote an edifying set of verses entitled "The Virtue of the Mass," by way of instruction for the laity. He tells his readers of the countless benefits they gain by hearing Mass, for which

he cites the testimony of the fathers and
tradition :

Alban for England, Saint Denis for France,
Blessed King Edmund for royal governance,
Thomas of Canterbury for his meek sufferance.
At Westminster Saint Edward shall not fail,
That none enemy shall hurt nor prevail,
But that Saint George shall make you freely pass,
Hold up your banner, in peace and in battail,
Each day when ye devoutly hear Mass.

Lydgate makes allusion to certain pious
beliefs which prevailed in England, as probably they still do in some Catholic countries. The first of these beliefs is that
devout attendance at Mass brings a signal
blessing upon temporal concerns in general :

Hearing of Mass giveth a great reward,
Ghostly health against all sickness . . . .
And unto folk that goen on pilgrimage,
It maketh them strong, getteth them secureness
Graciously to complete their voyage.
The mighty man, it maketh him more strong,
Recomforteth the sick in his langour,
Giveth patience to them that suffer wrong,
The labourer beareth up in his labour ;
To thoughtful folks, refreshing and succour,
Gracious counsel to folk disconsolate ;

Sustaineth the feeble, conveyeth the conqueror,
Maketh of merchants the fairs fortunate. . . .
Grace at departing, saith Saint John, to borrow ;
Good speed, good hap, in city, town and house,
To all that hear devoutly Mass at morrow.
Hearing of Mass doth passing great avail ;
At need and mischief, folk it doth relieve ;
Causeth Saint Nicholas to give good counsel,
And Saint Julian * good harbour at eve ;
Behold Saint Christopher,† no enemy shall thee
     grieve,
And Saint Loy ‡ your journey shall preserve.
Horse nor cart that day shall not mischieve,
Mass heard afore, who doth these saints serve.

Dan Lydgate is here writing what he terms
" A short Contemplation, after the opinion
of Saint Bernard, what virtue is in the hearing of Mass." His theme in general is, that
Mass, devoutly heard, brings temporal benefits, and particularly to wayfarers. This latter

---

* Saint Julian is the patron saint of innkeepers.

† Allusion is to the colossal picture of Saint
Christopher commonly painted on the north wall
of a parish church, opposite the south porch. To
look on it was believed to be a preservative
against sudden death on that day.

‡ Saint Eligius, as a worker in iron, is regarded
as a protector of blacksmiths, horses and carts.

point is capable of being carried further. In the Middle Ages there was a pious belief that no journey was shortened by the hearing of Mass ; * that angels guided and protected persons on their way to and from Mass ; nay, that the time spent at Mass was not deducted from the duration of any man's life :

Parting from Mass, 'ginning your journey,
Call on Saint Michael your pace to fortify,
For sudden haste and good prosperity ;
And for glad tiding, Saint Gabriel shall you guide ;
And Raphael, record of Tobye,†
Shall be your leech and your medicine.

A little further on, this note appears in the margin : "Words of Saint Austin touching the meeds of the Mass, so as it is ledged in *Fasciculus Morum* "—and Lydgate continues :

That day a man devoutly heareth Mass,
While he is present he shall not waxen old.
In going thither his steps, more and less,

---

* An old Welsh proverb ran : *Nid hwy y daith er gwrando Offeren*—"Not longer is the journey for the hearing of Mass."
† As witness Tobias.

Be of angels numbered and told. . . .
Hearing of Mass letteth no voyage,
As it hath well been proved in certain,
Prayer at Mass doth great advantage,
With Christ's Passion, to souls in their peyne.
The Mass also doth other things twain :
To soul and body giveth consolation ;
If he pass that day by death suddain,
Standeth for housel and his Communion.

    *   *   *   *   *   *

Mass heard afore, the wind is not contrary
To mariners that day, in their sailing. . . .
No time is lost during that service.
For which let no man plainly be in doubt,
But that God shall dispose in many wise
To increase all things that they gon about.

Let us now see the same idea worked
out in another composition. We will turn
from the Saxon to the Celtic race, and select
a Welsh poem written by the bard Ieuan ap
Rhydderch, about the year 1420. It is
entitled *Cywydd yr Offeren* *—" An Ode to
the Mass." The bard says :

" Many, by pure and blessed Saint Mary,
are the virtues of the Mass. He who hears
Mass devoutly will come to a good end.

---

* I have collated three different MSS. of this.

The man who is present thereat, God strengthen him, he will not grow old, he will not get too hot. A good angel will be at his side, numbering every step from his house to the fair church. If he should die suddenly as he stands, and there should be a lawsuit for his property, God will reward him, and his lord will find it difficult to take a pennyworth of his goods. . . . When Mass is spoken of, what sense or what word is adequate? It is to the soul eight kinds of medicine at once, all prosperity and all worthy protection; to the body true happiness."

Let us now turn to another old Welsh document. This is a fragment written in 1346, and entitled: *Rhinweddau Gwrando Offeren* *—" The Merits (or Virtues) of hearing Mass." It runs thus:

"The five merits (or virtues) of Sunday Mass are these: The first of them is, that the duration of thy life shall be the longer by

* "The Elucidarium and other Tracts in Welsh." Jones and Rhys. Oxford, Clarendon Press, 1894, p. 151.

that of every Mass thou ever hearest. The second is, that all thy unseasonable food of Sunday * shall be pardoned. The third is, that God will pardon all thy venial sins of Sunday. The fourth is, that when thou goest to get † Sunday Mass, it shall be the same to thee as if thou wert given from thy father's home as a true gift to God.‡   The fifth is, that if a man go to purgatory he shall have rest for the duration of every Mass he has heard."

The document then continues with what seem to be the same ideas in a different form : " The merits (or virtues) of seeing § the Body of Christ are these : When Mass is sung, thy unseasonable food is forgiven on the day thou seest It. Thy profitless conversation is not remembered against thee. For oaths sworn in ignorance thou shalt not be punished.   Sudden death shall not come

---

* The meaning is obscure.

† The phrase "to get Mass" is still common among English-speaking Catholics.

‡ A doubtful translation of an obscure passage.

§ This phrase will be explained later.

to thee that day. If thou die on the day
that thou seest It, the privilege of Communion shall be thine that day ; and this
because of taking Mass-bread.* Whilst thou
hearest Sunday Mass thou shalt not so long
grow older. Every step thou goest to get
Sunday Mass, an angel shall accompany
thee ; and for every step thou shalt have a
reward. No evil sprite shall abide with
thee whilst thou goest to Sunday Mass."

Then follows a stanza of poetry, evidently
of greater antiquity than the foregoing prose
text :

Of thy speech, Tyssul,† I will ask thee on thy
    mule :
What shall I do about Sunday Mass ?
If thou keep Sunday Mass through faith and be-
    lief and religion,
Blessed will they be that travel with thee.
Of thy speech, in earnest, I will ask thee, through
    attributes : ‡

* This point will be explained later.
† A saint of the old Cambro-British Church,
who has given his name to the parish of Llan-
dysilio-gogo.
‡ Doubtful translation of this word.

What shall I do if I be without it ?
If thou shalt be without it, without necessary
labour,
For the rest of that week see thou laugh not nor
smile.

We shall presently meet with a later and more intelligible version of this poem.

The reader will have noticed the occurrence in the above document of several ideas already found in the treatise of Dan Lydgate, namely, the idea of security from sudden death on the day that Mass has been heard, the arrest of advancing age while hearing Mass, and the fellowship of an angel and the acquisition of merit in every step on the way to Mass.

There is a curious and very ancient Welsh poem consisting of a dialogue between King Arthur and the Eagle—the bird of wisdom in British lore. Among many questions on weighty matters of religion, Arthur asks the Eagle : "O Eagle, a recondite parable shalt thou tell, without concealment : Is it good to get Mass on Sunday ? " The Eagle answers : " If thou shalt get Sunday

Mass, and water and bread after, blessed is thy state." The next question put by King Arthur is: "O Eagle, thou shalt manifest truly, chief in prudence, candle of prophets: What shall I do if I be without it?" Answer: " If thou shalt be without Mass on Sunday, without necessity on thee or compulsion, throughout the week see thou laugh not nor smile."

From this and the previous reference it seems clear that a pious belief prevailed in ancient times to the effect that culpable failure to attend Sunday Mass should be expiated by voluntary abstention from mirth until the Sunday following. Before leaving this branch of our subject, it will be interesting to note that the version of the above ode, printed in the " Myvyrian Archaiology of Wales," * has undergone a Protestant editing; the word " Mass " having been altered to "service," and the words "water and bread " to " grace from God "—thus robbing the stanzas of all their point. The allusion to bread and water shall be explained later.

* Gee, Denbigh, 1873, p. 132.

It is, perhaps, little wonder that our forefathers, profoundly impressed as they were
with the mystic sanctity and power of the
eucharistic rite, should have early come to
look upon the Mass as an invincible weapon
against malignant spirits.   Saint Augustine
mentions the laying of ghosts by the celebration of Mass in a haunted house.   The
writer of an old Welsh manuscript,* citing
this instance, moralizes thus : " You may see
the fruit of the Mass in the driving out of
devils, who are unable to endure the precious
Sacrifice "   On the other hand the ancient
fathers, as is well known, are fond of insist-
ing that angels surround the altar at the
moment of the consecration.   We have, also,
in the prayer at Mass, *Jube hæc perferri,* a
request that God will cause the offering to be
presented to Him " by the hands of Thy
holy angel "—the angel especially associated with the mysteries of the blessed
Eucharist.

In the collection of Welsh semi-mytho-

* Cardiff Free Library, MS. 17,119 (sixteenth
century).

logical stories known as the *Mabinogion*,*
dating, in their present form, from the
thirteenth century, the Celtic demi-god, Llew
Llaw Gyffes, confesses that he can be
wounded only by means of "a javelin
fashioned in a year's time and worked upon
solely during Sunday Mass."

Principal Rhys, Professor of Celtic at
Oxford University, in the course of his ethno-
logical researches in the Isle of Man, came
upon a tradition about Saint Maughold's
Well, to the effect that its water was good
for sore eyes, but "had its full virtue only
when visited the first Sunday of harvest, and
that only during the hour when the books
were open at church, which, shifted back to
Roman Catholic times, means doubtless the
hour when the priest was engaged in saying
Mass." † The learned author remarks that
he has heard similar virtue ascribed, with
the same restriction, to other wells in the

---

* Ed. Ivor B. John, M.A. ; London, Nutt, 1901,
p. 41.

† "Celtic Folklore, Welsh and Manx." Vol. I,
p. 315. Oxford, Clarendon Press. 1901.

Isle of Man, and even to the sea water there.

In a manuscript of the Llanover collection, of about the year 1610,* is a long list of dreams, 183 in number, with the interpretation of each. Two of them refer to the Mass. No. 9 tells us that to dream you see a priest donning his chasuble, "signifies something contrary." No. 14 says, however, that "To dream you see Mass being celebrated, is happiness."

A more eloquent tribute to the virtues of the holy Sacrifice is embodied in the Irish proverb: *Ni luach go h-Aiffrionn Dé éisteachd*—"There is no reward like hearing God's Mass."

Dan Lydgate wrote :

Ye folks all which have devotion
To hear Mass, first do your busy cure,
With all your inward contemplation,
As in a mirror, presenting in figure
The moral meaning of that ghostly armour . . . .
Call to your mind, of whole affection,

---

* In the handwriting of the Welsh antiquary-bard, Llewelyn Sion of Llangewydd, Glamorgan.

How that the Mass, here in this present life,
Of ghostly gladness is chief direction
To have memory of Christ's Passion . . . .
Against our ghostly sickness our restoration,
Our balm, our treacle,* health and medicine.

A correspondent of "Notes and Queries" (9th S. ix, 149) calls attention to a belief prevailing in the Vosges, that the direction of the wind during Midnight Mass of Christmas determines the predominant wind for the ensuing year. This is but one illustration of the mysterious awe with which the first Mass of Christmas Day has been from time immemorial regarded. As Scott sings :

This only night of all the year,
Saw the stoled priest the chalice rear.

But there is also a peculiar atmosphere of reverence surrounding the parochial Mass of this greatest of Christian festivals. What Catholic does not know well the unique sensation of delighted awe, of mingled smiles and tears, with which (at least in childhood) he has assisted at the High Mass of Christmas Day in his parish church?

* Antidote or remedy.

The festal array in which the church is
bedecked, the banners, the evergreen gar-
lands, the lighted tapers on the very rood-
screen, the best vestments worn by the
officiating clergy for this great occasion ; the
crib with its holy images of the Babe and
His Mother and Saint Joseph, and the ox
and ass; the short and cheerful sermon,
ending with the preacher's Christmas wishes ;
the festive harmonies of Novello's *Adeste
Fideles* sung (all but the last verse) at the
Offertory, and—perhaps most impressive of
all—the solemn Benediction after Mass, the
blessed Sacrament enthroned amid lights
and flowers, dimly seen through the cloud of
incense and the fog of a December morning,
while the last verse of the *Adeste* greets the
new-born King on His humble throne :

> Ergo qui natus die hodiernâ,
> Jesu, tibi sit gloria,
> Patris Æterni Verbum Caro factum !
>   Venite, adoremus Dominum.

During the course of the religious revolu-
tion of the sixteenth century, a German Protestant named Naogeorgus wrote in Latin a

doggrel sàtire on Catholic faith and practice. This was translated by an English Reforming rhymester called Barnaby Googe. His translation, printed in 1570 and entitled "The Popish Kingdom," was immensely popular among the English Puritans, both Anglican and Nonconformist. In 1880 this was reprinted; and the book, originally intended for and used as a means of pouring contempt upon the Church, is now exceedingly valuable to antiquaries of all creeds, from its minute description of the religious ceremonies and usages of our Catholic forefathers. This is how it describes the way in which the Mass was regarded in ancient times :

Their trust is always in the Mass, to this they
    only fly
In everything that toucheth them, and every
    jeopardy.
And is not this a goodly crew? they are per-
    suaded still,
What day they hear or see a Mass, to have no
    kind of ill. . . .
Mass opens heaven's gates, and doth deliver men
    from hell ;

Mass healeth all diseases, and doth sicknesses
     expel.
Mass doth relieve the burdened mind, and sins
     defaceth quite. . . .
Mass plucks the sinful soul from out the purgatory
     fire,
Mass comforteth th' afflicted sort, and makes them
     to aspire.
Mass washeth clean the mind, and makes the
     guilty conscience clear ;
Mass doth obtain the grace of God, and keeps
     his favour here ;
Mass driveth wicked devils hence, and overthrows
     the fiends ;
Mass bringeth angels good from high, and makes
     them faithful friends.
Mass doth defend the traveller from danger and
     disease ;
Mass doth preserve the sailing ship amid the
     raging seas.
Mass giveth store of corn and grain, and helpeth
     husbandry ;
Mass blesseth every such as seeks in wealthy state
     to be.
Mass gets a man a pleasant wife, and gets the
     maid her mate ;
Mass helps the captain in the field, and furthereth
     debate. . . .
Mass helps the hunter with his horn, and makes
     the dogs to run ;

Mass sendeth store of sport and game into their
    nets to come.

Mass mollifieth angry minds, and driveth rage
    away ;

Mass brings the woeful lovers to their long-desired
    day.

Mass doth destroy the witches' works, and makes
    their charmings vain. . . .

Mass makes thy prayers be heard, and giveth thy
    request ;

Mass drives away the greedy wolf that doth the
    sheep molest.

Mass makes the murrain for to cease, and stock
    to thrive apace ;

Mass makes thy journey prosper well, where'er
    thou turn'st thy face.

Mass overthrows thine en'my's force, and doth
    resist his might ;

Mass drives out Robin Goodfellow, and bugs *
    that walk by night.

Mass plague and hunger doth expel, and civil
    mutiny ;

Mass makes a man with quiet mind and con-
    science clear to die. . . .

In Mass is all their trust and strength, all things
    through Mass are done ;

In all their griefs and miseries, to Mass they
    straightways run.

* Bogies, ghosts.

I think we must do Master Googe the
justice of saying that these stanzas hardly
exaggerate the sentiment of Catholics toward
the Mass—at all events where the full current
of ancient feeling has not been slackened by
exposure to the freezing temperature of in-
difference and scepticism.   In thoroughly
Catholic lands at the present day, as in our
own before the Reformation, every under-
taking, every anxious aspiration is com-
mended to almighty God and His saints by
the hearing of Mass.   Mass is heard daily by
the devout in those countries, as it is, indeed, in this.   Our ancestors could no more
dispense with it than with their bodily food.
They realized the full significance of the
petition : *Panem nostrum quotidianum da
nobis hodie.*

III--Mass in the Penal Times

Having obtained a graphic picture of the
way in which the Mass was regarded by our
ancestors in the Middle Ages, we must turn
our attention to post-Reformation times. It
is a matter of common knowledge, how that
reforming kings, prelates and preachers in
this country saw in the Mass the pith and
core of Catholicity—or, as they termed it,
of " Popery."   It is no wonder, therefore,
that these people who, from many various
motives, desired to bring about the utter ex-
tirpation of the old state of things and to
establish a new order in religious matters—
it is no wonder, I say, that they early perceived the Mass to be the chief object for
their attacks and for their innovations.   It
was the Mass that mattered above and before
all ; for the Mass was in a manner the kernel
of Catholic faith and practice and, in the
eyes of the people, represented all that their
forefathers had held most sacred.   The Re-

formers made no secret of their conviction
that Catholicism could only be uprooted
from the popular mind and affection by
destroying the Mass and everything connected therewith.   I am writing on folklore,
not history, so it will be sufficient to refer to
the injunctions, straitly enforced by the
governments of Edward VI and Elizabeth,
for the removal and destruction throughout
the realm of altars and altar-stones, patens
and chalices, pyxes and monstrances, cha-
subles, maniples and humerals, missals and
graduals—in short, everything connected
with the Sacrifice of the Mass and the doctrine of the Real Presence.   How thoroughly
these injunctions were obeyed is eloquently
witnessed by the extreme rarity of ancient
English-made examples of the objects above
referred to.

The establishment of Protestantism meant
for Catholics the commencement of the penal
times—that long period when to celebrate
Mass, or even to harbour a priest, was to in-
cur the guilt and the horrible punishment of
high treason; when the priest-hunter flou-

rished, and the priest's hiding-hole was constructed in many a noble mansion throughout the country; when gibbet, and cauldron
and disembowelling-knife awaited captured
priests in every county town. It might be
supposed that in that awful time of trial the
Mass was put down throughout the length
and breadth of the land. But this would be
to reckon without the unconquerable devotion of Catholic hearts to the Sacrament of
Love, that mystic rite which is the special
solace of the faithful in the time of tribula-
tion. Never has the Mass been so highly
prized, so worthily appreciated, or so devoutly approached as in the time when to
kneel at the altar was to court fines, im-
prisonment and death ; when non-attendance
at the Protestant service cost £20 * a month
to our Catholic gentry, and to our Catholic
poor all that they possessed.

The ravages of the Reformation, while
involving the demolition of many a chancel
as a logical sequence to the destruction of
the high altar, had a further effect, which has

---

* = five or six times present value.

perhaps not received from historians and
antiquaries the attention it deserves.   I
allude to the dismantling and abandonment
of a large number of small chapels, one of
which, at least, was to be found in nearly
every parish.   These chapels, standing sometimes by the highway, sometimes almost
hidden in a wood, or crowning some isth-
mus on the coast, were often of greater antiquity than the parish church.   They were,
for the most part, used only occasionally—
some only for Mass on the anniversary of
their dedication.   The more important of
these little old chapels (especially such as
had tithes or offerings assigned for their
maintenance) were snapped up in the general
scramble for Church property ; but numbers
were simply left to fall into decay, and it is
with them that we are here concerned.
These abandoned shrines were very often
used by the persecuted priests for the celebration of Mass, and also for a stealthy performance of marriages, christenings and
burials, usually at dead of night.   On the
arrival of some hunted priest at a Catholic

mansion, word would be cautiously sent to
persons who were known to be devout
Catholics. At the hour appointed the adhe-
rents of the ancient faith, after creeping
along from their homes, by hedges and
ditches, or along half-forgotten Roman
roads, would gather at the ruined chapel.
The door would be shut and barred, and a
trusty watcher left on guard outside to give
timely warning of the approach of danger.
Quickly the priest would produce a portable
altar-stone and don his vestments, while the
clerk or server would light the pair of tapers.
The chalice and paten would be brought,
perhaps, from the mansion of the Catholic
squire. Then, in the dim light, with no
sound but the night wind to break upon the
whispered prayers of priest and clerk, the
Host would be raised as of old ; while the
little congregation kneeled in fear and
trembling, but proud and happy at being
gathered together with our Lord in their
midst.

Traces of such a chapel still exist at the
north-eastern extremity of the Skyrrid moun-

tain, near Abergavenny. It was dedicated
under the invocation of Saint Michael, and
gave to the Sgiryd Fawr the alternative
names of Saint Michael's or the Holy
Mountain. Evidence was given in 1678,
before a Commission of enquiry into Popery
in Monmouthshire and Herefordshire,* to
the effect that the Papists met in that hill-
chapel eight or ten times a year, where Mass
was said and sometimes sermons preached.
A hundred Papists had been seen there at
a time. The place was described as a
ruinous chapel. It contained a stone with
crosses on it, which an informer correctly
took to be an altar-stone. He had seen
people with beads in their hands, kneeling
towards the said stone both within and
without the chapel. He had been informed
that Mass was often said there.

In the town of Abergavenny (so Mr John
Arnold, magistrate and priest-hunter, re-
ported to the Commission) there was a

---

* "An Abstract of several Examinations,"
etc. London, 1680. (Recently reprinted for sub-
scribers.)

public chapel near the Priory, the house of
Mr Thomas Gunter, a convicted Papist.
This chapel was "adorned with the marks
of the Jesuits on the outside"—the sacred
monogram I.H.S.—and Mass was said there
by "Captain Evans," a reputed Jesuit. (This
was the Ven. Philip Evans, S.J., martyred at
Cardiff in 1679.) The Jesuit Father David
Lewis, *recte* Charles Baker, also said Mass
there.* Arnold further reports that "great
numbers resort to the said chapel; and he
hath credibly heard that a hundred had
gone out of the said chapel, when not forty
have gone out of the great church."

Perhaps the most curious illustration of
the strength of "Popery" in Monmouthshire
during the reign of Charles II and James II
is furnished by a document in a bundle of
Recusant Papers 1688-1717, at the London
Record Office. It is dated 1689 and is a
schedule of lands and tenements which were
found to have been assigned to "supersti-
tious uses" in the county of Monmouth.

---

* He was martyred in 1679 at Usk, and is
buried in the churchyard there.

It states that the ancient chapel of Llanfair
in the parish of Llantilio Croseny, adjoining
the mansion of Thomas Croft, esquire, was
not only used for Mass and other Popish
services, but that the priest actually collected
the tithes belonging to the said chapel, in
that and two adjoining parishes ! *

The same document records that a certain house and twenty acres of land called
" Tyers Uffrinall," in the parish of Llanishen
in the said county of Monmouth, was conveyed for the benefit and maintenance of
priests of the Church of Rome.   The name
of this land, as above copied, can only be
intended for the Welsh words " Tir Offere-
nol," meaning the Mass Land—a term indi-
cative of the principal end and object of the
donation referred to.

A document preserved among the Cecil
MSS. at Hatfield House contains a curious
account of a discovery of " Mass stuff " at an
old mansion in Yorkshire, after the removal

---

* The ruins of this chapel still exist, and were
long used as a burial-place for the numerous
Catholic families of the neighbourhood.

of the rightful and Catholic owners. Here
it is:

"*Cecil Papers.* Vol. 191, No. 92. From
Huddington. W. Walsh and E. Newport to
Sir R. Walsh. December 4, 1605.

"Some of your servants now remaining
at Huddington, and having charge there by
your command, hath of late discovered a
hollow place within a wall near unto the
clock house, which hath not formerly been
perceived. Whereupon your lady requested
us to ride thither and to search the said
place, which thing we have done with all
diligence according to our duties; and there
we found a cross gilt, with the picture of
Christ and other pictures upon it, a chalice
of silver parcel gilt, with a little plate or
cover to the said chalice, and certain boxes
of singing-bread,* and all other ornaments
fit for a Popish priest to say Mass in; and
certain Popish Mass-books, most of them in
Latin and some in English, to the number
of fifty or threescore, whereof some are newly
printed."

Mass-wafers.

Another Monmouthshire document* preserved at the Record Office supplies us with an interesting statement, dated 1686, of a piece of robbery enacted by a notorious priest-finder, the lieutenant of John Arnold. It was found that Charles Price of Llanffoist, esquire, had in his possession "severall peices of plate fformerly belonging to mr David Lewis a Jesuite who was condemned and executed for the late pretended Popish Plott." The articles in question were:

> One large silver and gilt chalice and paten.
> One small plain silver chalice and paten.
> One pair of small silver flower-pots.
> One silver thurible and cover.
> One small silver plate for cruets.
> One silver cruet.
> One silver bell for the altar.
> One small pair of silver candlesticks.
> Several small pieces of silver formerly belonging to a crucifix.

---

* Exchequer Proceedings, Monmouthshire, etc., 3 Jac. II, No. 6743.

> One picture of the Virgin Mary, with
> a silver and gilt inner frame.

These were the modest vessels and ornaments which were found on the altar when
the Ven. Charles Baker (*alias* David Lewis)
was seized in the act of preparing to celebrate Mass in a house at Llantarnam, Monmouthshire, in 1679.

In the same terrible year of persecution
there was a seizure of Mass-stuff at the Cwm,
on the Herefordshire side of the Monnow
Valley, three miles north of Monmouth.
The Cwm had long been a secret mission-
centre of the Jesuits. The authorities obtained information as to the priests who said
Mass there, " but the altar with all the ornaments thereof was taken down and conveyed
away; only the altar-stone remaining, with
five crosses cut in it, one at each corner and
one in the middle." These were, of course,
the consecration crosses. In the neighbour-
ing wood the raiders found two sets of vestments in boxes, and, in the " pig's cote,"
about two horse-loads of books in English

and Welsh. They also discovered "bottles
of oil," a box of Mass-wafers, sundry pictures,
crucifixes, relics, a little "saint's bell" and
an incense pot.*

The "Abstract of Several Examinations,"
dated 1680, from which I have already
quoted, also contains the evidence of an
informer named John Scudamore,† an apo-
state; who says that he apprehended one
Mr William Elliot, a Popish priest, habited
in his vestments, in the act of celebrating
Mass in a chapel in Herefordshire; wherein
he observed an altar, lights and images. He
asked the said Elliot how he durst say Mass
so publicly—there being at Mass above thirty
persons. This priest was committed to
Hereford gaol, but was afterwards removed
to the Tower of London, whence he was
liberated by the King's warrant. The Stuart
sovereigns were always willing to save a

* "A Short Narrative of the Discovery of a
College of Jesuits," etc., 1679.

† This unhappy man betrayed the Ven. John
Kemble, priest, who was put to death at Hereford
in 1679.

priest's life, when they could do so without attracting the attention of the Puritans.

From very ancient times it has been the custom of the Catholic gentry to maintain private chapels in their country mansions. Episcopal and sometimes papal licence is requisite, however, before Mass may be celebrated, or the Blessed Sacrament reserved in a private chapel ; and such licence is not readily granted.

In 1395 Elizabeth Bottreaux successfully petitioned her diocesan, the Bishop of Exeter, for licence to have Mass celebrated in her domestic chapel of Saint Mary Magdalen at Boswithguy, in the parish of Saint Erth, in the county of Cornwall.* This privilege, after being several times renewed, was finally, in 1411, extended to all the mansions held by John Bottreaux and Elizabeth his wife within the diocese.

In 1332 William Maelog, Lord of Llys-

---

* Indices to the Registers of the ancient Bishops of Exeter, by Prebendary Hingeston-Randolph, cited in Matthews' History of the Borough of Saint Ives.

talybont, near Cardiff, and his wife, vainly
endeavoured to enforce in the Court of the
Bishop of Llandaff a claim to have Mass
said "at their house on the other side of the
Taf," at Christmas and Easter. They alleged
an ancient grant by the Bishop and Chapter
in consideration of certain lands given to the
see by their ancestors.*

Manifold were the consolations afforded
to the afflicted faithful by the chapels of our
Catholic mansions, during two hundred years
of almost incessant persecution.

Raglan Castle, in Monmouthshire, was
the last stronghold (except Scilly) to hold
out for King Charles I against the forces of
Cromwell and Fairfax.   But it boasts a still
greater honour, that of having housed, on
the altar of its chapel, the King of kings
under His sacramental veil, from the com-
pletion of the structure in the fifteenth century to the year 1646, when the loyal and
heroic defenders marched out with all the
honours of war.   Down to that unhappy
day Mass had been daily sung, and the rites

* "Cardiff Records," vol. II, p. 20, citing the
Liber Landavensis.

of the Ancient Church regularly performed
in the chapel of Raglan Castle—even in the
penal times   In Kenelm Digby's *Broad
Stone of Honour* we read an interesting
story of a woman, said to be over a hundred
years old, who remembered the Catholic
worship in Queen Mary's reign, and who
was conveyed by the Earl of Worcester to
Raglan Castle in order that she might be
able to hear Mass every day. Her delight
was so great that she died soon after,
literally killed by joy at being so privileged.

By far the greater number of the families
of gentry in Monmouthshire were Catholic
down to the eighteenth century, by the end
of which most of them had either died out
in the male line, or had been reduced, by
fines and confiscation for recusancy, to the
condition of poor yeomanry. Nearly every
mansion had its private chapel for the celebration of Mass whenever a priest could be
obtained; and many of them had secret
hiding-chambers for the hunted clergy.*
Secluded pathways (still often called "the

* Treowen, in the parish of Dingastow, has
three hiding-chambers most artfully constructed.

church-way ") * were known to the Catholics
in the neighbourhood of every such country
seat, enabling the domestic chapel to be
approached from the various homesteads
where dwelled the scattered faithful. These
thought nothing of long nocturnal marches
to reach the place where Mass was to be
celebrated. They would start at midnight,
skirt the hedgerows to avoid observation,
and at daybreak leave their lanthorns at
some friendly house on the way, to be called
for on the evening journey homeward.

Among the invaluable Welsh manuscripts
of the Llanover collection is one in the
handwriting of William Pugh of Penrhyn in
North Wales, a Catholic physician, who
died in Monmouthshire in 1680 and was, I
strongly suspect, a missionary priest. This
book is a collection of poems and prose
writings, mostly of a devotional character,
intensely Catholic in tone and sentiment.

* A case in point is the paved path leading
across the river Monnow and the fields from Monmouth to Perthîr, where, in the mansion of the
Powel family, was a chapel long used by the
Monmouth Catholics.

Some of them are original compositions of the writer; and of these one of the most noteworthy is a poem entitled *Ni a gawn ein byd yn wyn*—" We shall be happy then." The author writes as a zealous Royalist, lamenting the exile of his lawful sovereign and the consequent miseries in Church and State; and he paints in anticipation a word-picture of the time when the old order of things shall be restored. His phraseology, however, is ingeniously adapted to a hidden meaning; and its inner significance is the restoration of the King who was exiled from His throne upon the now desecrated altar of the parish church. When holy Mass should again be chanted, and the King return "under a golden veil," then would Wales rejoice and the world be beautiful once more. The whole poem is extremely touching and inspiriting, and picturesquely illustrates the profound attachment of the former population to their ancient faith, and in particular to the Mass and the Blessed Sacrament.

No less loyal to the ancient Church and

to her great Sacrifice, than the people of
Monmouthshire, were the inhabitants of a
great portion of the county of York ; and it
is of interest to remember that the last time
Mass was publicly performed in any of the
ancient churches of England, namely, during
the Catholic rising of 1570, this honour fell
to Yorkshire.   Not only was High Mass
then sung in the cathedral of Durham, but
Mass was said also in the parish churches of
Staindrop, Darlington and Ripon, and probably at Stokesby and Whitby.

The old missionary priests in penal
times urgently impressed upon their har-
rassed flocks the necessity of two great devotions—to the Mass and to the Holy Souls.
In those days attendance at the Eucharistic
rite was a privilege so rarely to be had, and
so highly prized, that the celebrant, by the
desire of his congregation, would say Mass
(if time permitted) very slowly, making it
last an hour or so, that the faithful should
enjoy to the full a happiness which might
not soon fall to their lot again.   So great
was   the   devotion   of   the   people   that

they assisted at Mass with tears of pious joy.

If we are to believe (and what Catholic will doubt it?) the old Yorkshire proverb, "God loves them that love the Mass," the good Catholics of this county are dear to our Lord. It is said that a Yorkshire husbandman named Davidson used to walk a great distance from his home at Rickle to chapel, taking with him his infant children, whom he carried by turns, in order that, as he expressed it, they might "have the benefit of the Mass."

Old-fashioned Yorkshire Catholics still speak of "going to prayers" when they mean going to Mass. This, of course, has come down from the times when it was not safe to refer to the Holy Sacrifice under its ordinary name.*

Another relic still sometimes to be met with, of the days of persecution, is the

---

* For these fragments of the folklore of his native county I am indebted to my friend Mr H. H. Spink, junior, of York, author of "The Gunpowder Plot and Lord Mounteagle's Letter."

4

practice, in country missions, of shutting
the chapel door just before the Consecration
at Mass and opening it after the Communion. I am told this was recently the
custom at Courtfield, near Ross; and I have
myself seen it done at Alfreton, Derbyshire,
in the eighties of the nineteenth century.
At such primitive places the attendance of
Protestant strangers at Mass was rather re-
sented by the Catholic rustics.

At Courtfield, and probably in other
rural missions, an offering is frequently
made to the priest for Mass to be said for
the safe delivery of cows, ewes or mares.
The offering of Mass for such private inten-
tions is ancient and eminently Catholic.

IV—Mass Vestments and Church Furniture

Wherever an historic priesthood exists, whether in the Catholic Church or in the separated communions of the East, there is one and one only sacrificial robe worn by the *sacerdos* in celebrating Mass, and that is the vestment called in Latin *planeta*, or *casula* ("houselet"), English "chasuble," French *chasuble*, Italian *pianeta*, Spanish *casulla*, Welsh *casul*.

The chasuble was originally an ample round garment, with a hole in the middle. It thus differs from the cope (a non-eucharistic vestment) in being undivided, while the cope is parted in front.

A quaint legend was related in connection with the chasuble of Saint Dunstan, the great restorer of English monasticism. His Life by Eadmer * tells us that the saint,

* "Memorials of Saint Dunstan." Rolls Series. 1874.

once thinking to hand his chasuble, after
Mass, to a minister, and not observing the
latter's absence, the chasuble remained suspended in the air. This chasuble was preserved at Westminster, and the people loved
to tell how Saint Dunstan "hung his vestment
on a sunbeam." He is said to have appeared
in a vision to a sick lady, and told her to put
an orfrey to his chasuble.   She did so, and
recovered at once from her illness.

The Catholic church of Saint Mary in the
town of Monmouth possesses a beautiful
storied chasuble of the fourteenth century.
It is of crimson velvet adorned with cloth of
gold.   The cross on the back and the orfrey
in front are needleworked, embroidered with
figures, in gold and colours, of the Crucifix,
our Lady, Saint John Evangelist and other
saints, in Gothic canopies. This vestment
was used in the time when the Monmouth
mission was united with that of Holywell,
Flintshire ; and tradition says that the Jesuit
missioners in the penal times carried it with
them on their perilous journeyings.   It then
had a lining of coarse canvas, or sacking ;

and the itinerant priest, disguised as a
labourer, wore it over his shoulders inside
out.

Among other treasures ot ecclesiastical
antiquity at the Monmouth church are two
very ancient processional crosses ; also the
altar, chalice and missal used by the Ven.
John Kemble, the octogenarian martyr-priest,
at Pembridge Castle, Herefordshire, where he
was chaplain to the Scudamore family previous to his execution at Hereford in 1679.

In the British Isles, France, and some
other countries, the chasuble bears the large
cross embroidered on the back ; but in Italy
and elsewhere the cross is worked on the
front of the chasuble.   The Ven. Thomas à
Kempis wrote as though, in his time in
Flanders, the cross was borne on both sides:
" He bears before and behind the sign of his
Lord's cross, that he may always remember
the Passion of Christ." *

The other distinctively eucharistic vestment is the maniple, a strip of stuff worn on

* "The Imitation of Christ."   Book IV,
chap. v.

the celebrant's left arm at Mass. In the
Hereford " use " (by a curious exception) the
maniple was worn out of Mass, namely, in
celebrating espousals in the church porch.

We must not omit a reference to the
pallium, which is, in some sort, an eucharistic
vestment, though it is in the first place a
symbol of metropolitan episcopal jurisdiction.
It will not be necessary here to go into the
history or the full significance of the pallium.
Suffice it to say that this garment is a long,
thin strip of white lamb's wool, marked with
several black crosses and slightly weighted at
each end by a small disc of lead.   It is
worn by archbishops only, as an almost abso-
lute rule, and chiefly when celebrating Ponti-
fical High Mass on certain great feasts.   The
following is a translation* of the words with
which Pope John XII, in the year 960, con-
ferred the pallium upon Saint Dunstan, Archbishop of Canterbury, in Rome :

" We give to your fraternity the pallium,
to be used according to custom at the cele-

* From the original Latin in "Memorials of
Saint Dunstan," Rolls series, 1874.

bration of Mass ; and We grant you the use
thereof—the privileges of your church remaining in their present state—not otherwise
than at the Nativity of our Lord and at the
Epiphany, at the Resurrection and Ascension of our Lord, and at Pentecost, as also
at the Assumption of Mary, the Mother of
God, or on the feasts of the apostles; also in
the consecration of bishops, and on your own
birthday (i.e. consecration day), and on the
day of the consecration of a church ; which
use Our predecessors established."

This will be an appropriate stage at which
to make some observations upon the ancient
arrangement and furniture of an ordinary
parish church.   The high altar, standing in
the rounded apse, but not contiguous with
the east wall at its rear, was backed by a
reredos carved with images of saints in pa-
nelled and canopied compartments.   Often,
either in place of or in addition to the reredos, there was a triptych painted with such
subjects as the Crucifixion or the Epiphany
on the centre panel, and the Annunciation
and the Ascension on the right and left.

A crucifix and two pricket candlesticks
stood on the altar.   A permanent tabernacle forming a structural portion of the
altar was exceptional; the usual arrangement being either *(a)* a dove-shaped pyx of
silver, suspended above the altar by a chain
from the roof, or *(b)* an aumbry or square
recess in the north wall of the chancel,
having a strong door secured by a lock.
In Germany the latter arrangement developed into what is termed a *Sakramentshaus-
lein*—"Sacrament's houselet"—a separately-
constructed receptacle of carved stone, surmounted by a crocketed and highly ornamented pinnacle towering aloft to the roof
on the north side of the chancel.   The
hanging lamp with its perpetually-burn-
ing light then, as now, indicated the
Divine Presence in the sanctuary.

The sides of the altar, north and south,
were screened by hangings of rich diapered
stuff, the colour of which, like the silken
altar-frontal, varied according to the day.

On the epistle side of the chancel, in
the south wall, was an arched recess

containing the piscina and the credence
shelf. Just west of this was usually a triple
seat of stone, called *sedilia*, elaborately
carved in a deep recess of the south wall of
the chancel, for the priest, deacon and subdeacon at High Mass. These arrangements
have been commonly reproduced in churches
built during the present revival of Gothic
architecture.

The chancel was divided from the nave
by a wall pierced with an arch, under which
were one or two steps and the rood-screen—
a structure of wood or stone which supported
a narrow gallery called the rood-loft. Along
one side of the loft, across the chancel arch,
ran the rood-beam, from which rose the rood,
or large crucifix, flanked on the north by an
image of our Lady, and south by a corres-
ponding effigy of Saint John Evangelist. The
foot of the rood was fixed on the rood-beam,
on which also were sockets or prickets for
candles called rood-lights. The rood-screen
usually consisted of two or more joists up-
holding the rood-loft and combined wlth two
or more arches. The joists rested upon a

dwarf wall, in the centre of which, under the
middle arch of the screen, was the chancel
door of wood or metal.   This door was often
so constructed as to shut at an obtuse angle
with its point inwards towards the altar, and
to open with the mere pressure against it of
the body of the crucifer or cross-bearer, as he
headed the procession into the chancel. The
most minute detail of church construction in
those days had its eucharistic symbolism ;
and this peculiarity of the door between
nave and chancel was held to signify the
ready access to almighty God and to the
heavenly kingdom which is secured to
mankind by the institution of the holy
Eucharist.   The lower panels of the rood-
screen were filled in with paintings of saints
and angels, in rich colours on a gold
background—thus connecting the mediæval rood-screen with its eastern counter-
part, the *iconostasis* of churches of the
Oriental rites.

The rood-loft was reached from the nave
by a narrow door and stone staircase in a
turret, close to the chancel arch.   At the

head of the stair one stepped through another door on to the loft.

The use of the rood-loft was to hold the organ and the choir, and to afford a convenient position for making announcements to the congregation and for the performance of certain ritual functions of occasional occurrence. Moreover, it was from the rood-loft that the deacon chanted the Gospel at High Mass.

Sometimes there was a small altar in the rood-loft itself ; oftener there was one under the loft, on the west side of the screen. Occasionally there were two such rood-screen altars, north and south—as still to be seen in the renascence church of Saint Jacques at Antwerp.

At Saint Ives, Cornwall, the rood staircase turret is still called the " organ tower " —a reminiscence of the days when the organ stood in the rood-loft. In this country, the finest examples of rood screens which iconoclasm has spared are at Patrishio and Llangwm in the county of Monmouth. Painted screen-panels are most frequent in Norfolk.

In the case of such a highly elaborate rood-screen as that of Llangwm, the congregation can have seen but little of the high altar, and can only have had glimpses of the ceremonial.   To this day, in churches of the Oriental rites, the altar is almost entirely hidden from the public gaze by the *iconostasis*, which consists of a solid wall between chancel and nave, broken only by the arch. Even this narrow opening is closed from the consecration to the priest's communion by a veil drawn across it.

Oaken seats and kneeling-benches were the rule in this country in mediæval times. The ends of them were often very elaborately and beautifully carved.   One of the black oak bench-ends at Saint Ives, Cornwall, is surmounted by the figure of a kneeling angel, habited in cassock and surplice and holding a pyx.   It was only in exceptional cases that a particular seat was reserved for the use of a family or an individual ; but the constant custom of occupying a particular place in the church often secured to a person a prescriptive right thereto.   People used to take can-

dles with them to church to give light at
early Mass. These candles they stuck on to
the ledge in front of the seat, to read their
missals and primers by. Primers were ver-
nacular books of devotion for Mass and
Office.

Quarrels between parishioners, about the
use of particular seats, were not uncommon,
and sometimes even resulted in free fights
in church or churchyard. From a record of
of Star Chamber proceedings instituted by
Richard Berrow, gentleman, of Gloucester-
shire, we get a glimpse of such a dispute.
Berrow stated that he was the owner of the
manor of Field Court in the parish of
Hardwick. The manor being, however,
nearer to the parish church of Quedgeley,
he attended the latter, and was accustomed
to use a certain sitting there. On Sunday,
the last day of June, 1533, as the priest was
saying Matins openly in the said church,
between 9 and 10 o'clock in the forenoon,
one Nicholas Arnold of Hingham, gentleman, came up to the place where complai-
nant was kneeling at prayers, and ordered

him to go away. He declined to go, and
remained at his place until Matins and
High Mass were ended. A witness for the
defence deposed that Mr Berrow had rudely
persisted in leaning forward over the back
of the seat in which one Mistress Alice
Porter sate, on purpose to annoy her and
her husband. Berrow stated that Arthur
Porter of Quedgeley, gentleman, had caused
a form or block of timber, upon which he,
the said plaintiff, usually did kneel or sit,
to be removed from the place where it was
wont to be, to another place in the said
church. Also that Mr Porter's servants,
by command of their master, tied a dog in
the seat or place of plaintiff's wife; and that
the said Porter came to Quedgeley church
on the eve of Lady Day last, and told
certain persons to keep the said Richard
Berrow out of his seat in the said church.*

As is incidentally mentioned in the above
document, the High Mass of Sundays and
great feasts was preceded by the public

* Star Chamber proc., Hen. 8, vol. III, fo.
163-8.

liturgical singing of Matins.   We may remark here that, in the Middle Ages, most
people of average intelligence were able to
join in the chanting of the Latin psalms,
anthems, responses, hymns and sequences
of the Divine Office and of the Mass, and
did so with great fervour.   The singing
was performed antiphonally by choir and
people, chanting alternately, in the plain-
song proper to the feast or fast of each day.

We have referred to the mediæval practice
of reserving the Blessed Sacrament within a
dove-shaped pyx of precious metal, suspended
over the altar by a chain from the roof.
That this was the general custom down to
the Reformation appears by a passage in a
Welsh MS.* defence of Catholic doctrine
against Protestants, written in the reign of
Elizabeth : " It may be seen that Saint Basil,
in the first honourable Œcumenical Council of
Nicæa, after consecrating gave a portion of
the Body of Christ to be kept in a golden
dove which hung above the altar, like the
pyx nowadays."

* Cardiff Free Library, Philipps MS. 17,119.

The same Welsh manuscript contains a story of a kind which was in favour in those times of bitter controversy, about a certain heretic who, for denying the Real Presence, was summoned "before the Archbishop of Canterbury and other Lords, and many of the Commons, at the church of St Paul in London. There the heretic was commanded to adore Christ in the Host. Then began the man to rail against Christ in the Host, answering that a spider deserved more reverence than Christ in the Host. Immediately after these words, all the people saw a huge spider start from the ceiling of the church, spinning his line towards the blasphemer's mouth, and trying to enter straightway into those poisonous lips."

V.-The Ordinary and Canon of the Mass

Although the Canon of the Mass remains substantially what it was in primitive ages, the Ordinary of the Mass (i.e., the portions which precede the *Te igitur* and follow the Communion) has undergone some modifications in the course of centuries. Thus a ceremony which, in the earlier Middle Ages, was a striking feature of the beginning of the eucharistic rite, has in the lapse of time become reduced to very modest proportions. I allude to the procession, or solemn entrance of the clergy chanting the Litanies, the celebrant carrying the book of the Gospels. More will be said about this later on. We will now turn to what is still an essential part of every Mass, namely, the

Kyrie eleison

This pathetic nine-fold appeal to the Divine mercy is an instance of the retention of Greek phrases in the Latin rite, which is

5

said to have for its object the maintenance
of a liturgical link between West and East.

It was said of St Dunstan that when he
said Mass he often heard invisible choirs of
angels singing the *Kyrie eleison.*   In his day
it was the custom for the Archbishop of
Canterbury, on Sundays and great feasts, to
sing a Mass which was attended by the King.
One Sunday the King went hunting early in
the morning, and kept Dunstan waiting to
begin Mass.   As the holy archbishop was
standing silently before the altar in his vestments, he saw Mass celebrated in heaven,
and heard the choirs of angels sing *Kyrie
eleison*, and so on to the *Ite, missa est.*   Just
then the royal clerks came hastening in to
say that the King was at hand ; but Dunstan
refused to say Mass, and doffed his vestments, at the same time enjoining upon the
King never again to hunt on Sundays.   The
heavenly *Kyrie* which Dunstan heard that
day he taught to his clerics ; and the same,
says his biographer, is still sung in many
churches.   It is called *Kyrie Rex Splendens*,
and, without verses, occurs in the Sarum

Missal, between the Introit and the Collect.*

Dan Lydgate says, in the course of his treatise which we have so often quoted from :

Kyrie and *Christe,* in number thrice three,
Words of Greek, plainly to determine,
Of mercy, calling to the Trinity
His ghostly grace, His people to illumine.
The number is token of the Orders Nine,
Our orisons and prayers to present
To Jesus Christ, most gracious and benign.

Gloria in Excelsis, next in order sung,
Token of unity and perfect peace,
At Christ's birth heard in Latin tongue
High in the air, by angels doubtless.

---

* *Cantus qui vocatur Kyrie Rex Splendens.* " In festo S. Michaelis in mense Septembris dicitur Kyrie Rex Splendens cum suis versibus ; in festo S. Dunstani et S. Michaelis in Monte Tumba dicitur Kyrie Rex absque versibus.

" Kyrie Rex Splendens cœli arce salve jugiter, et clemens plebi tuæ semper eleyson. . . .

" Virginis piæ Mariæ o alma Proles, Rex re gum, benedicte Redemptor, cruore mercatis proprio mortis ex potestate semper eleyson. "

The above is an example of the "farced" Kyries which obtained in some places in the Middle Ages, but have long since been disallowed.

Gloria in Excelsis

This is a hymn of joy, and so is omitted (except on special feasts) in Advent and from Septuagesima to Easter. It is, of course, also absent from Masses of Requiem.

The feast of Easter opens with the first *Alleluia* of Holy Saturday. When the celebrant intones *Gloria in excelsis* at the one Mass of Holy Saturday, the altars, images and pictures are instantly unveiled, the organ peals forth after its Lenten silence, and at the same moment the bells also find their voices again and ring out together joyously— from the tinkling brass one on the altar-step to the biggest bell in the tower.

In Malta, when the Mass of Holy Saturday is commencing, the boys assemble on the rocks by the sea shore, undress, and stand on the brink of the water. The moment the church bells ring out at the *Gloria in excelsis* every boy jumps into the sea and takes his first swim of the year.

Dominus Vobiscum

After the *Gloria in excelsis* has been
said or sung, the priest kisses the altar,
and then turns to the people, saying:
Dominus vobiscum—" The Lord be with
you "; to which the clerk or the choir responds: *Et cum spiritu tuo*—" And with thy
spirit." This action, accompanied by these
words, occurs five times in the course of the
Mass, namely, thrice before the *Sanctus* and
twice after the Communion.

A sixteenth-century Welsh manuscript in
the Llanover collection * contains a short
but interesting piece headed *Paham y tryr
offairad i wyneb bvmwaith at y bobl, yn yr
offeren*—" Why the priest turns his face five
times towards the people in the Mass." It
proceeds thus: " Because our Lord Jesus
Christ appeared five times in this world
after His Passion:

---

* *Welsh Prose Miscellanea*, Glamorgan. Handwriting of Llewelyn Sion of Llangewydd.   End
of sixteenth century.

" Firstly, He appeared to Saint Mary of Maudlen.

" The second time, to the two disciples on the way, when they knew Him by the breaking of bread.

" The third time, to Saint Peter.

" The fourth time, He descended in the midst of His disciples, when He said : *Pax vobis*, that is, ' Peace be to you.'

" The fifth time, when He came amongst His twelve apostles and upbraided them for their unbelief in Him."

Lydgate sees the same significance in this ritual act, for he writes :

At the Postcommunion the priest doth him remue,
On the right side saith *Dominus vobiscum ;*
Five times the people doth salue
During the Mass, as made is mention.
Figure, the day of His Resurrection,
Five times He soothly did appear
To His disciples, for their consolation—
And first of all to His Mother dear.
Salve, sancta parens, He to His Mother said,
Which was to her rejoicing sovereign.

The Collect

Then is said by the celebrant a prayer called the Collect; or there may be, on feasts of minor rank and on ferials, two or more collects, according to the calendar. The general character of these prayers is well stated by Lydgate thus:

The priest at Mass shall say an Orison
For living people ; that they may, ere they die,
Have repentance, shrift and Communion ;
Souls in peyne, release and pardon ;
Grace through all nations, love and charity ;
Patience to folks in prison ;
Help to all needy, that live in poverty.

The Collect was, in the Middle Ages, called "The Orison;" a term which indicates the importance of this prayer, just as the name "vestment," then applied to the chasuble alone, marked it out as the sacerdotal garment *par excellence*.

The Epistle

At High Mass the Epistle is chanted by the subdeacon, in a monotone with a rise and fall of one note on the last two syllables of the lesson.   Distinguished from the Gospel, the Epistle represents the old dispensation and the synagogue.   As Lydgate writes :

> The Epistle is a token and figure,
> As say doctors, of law and prophecy
> Of Christ's coming, by evident Scripture ;
> As patriarchs afore did specify,
> And Baptist John, son of Zachary.
> And semblably, so as the morrow gray
> Is messenger of Phœbus' uprising,
> And bringeth tidings of the glad day—
> So the Epistle, by process of reading,
> To us declareth most gracious tiding
> Of the Gospel. . . .

Of the matter read by the priest between Epistle and Gospel, the most usual (according to the calendar) is the Gradual, called in olden English speech the " Grayle."   This begins and ends with *Alleluia*, whether it

be Paschal time or not. Lydgate's lines run
as follows :

> After th' Epistle, next followeth the Grayel,
> Token of ascending up from gree to gree ; *
> The ground first taken at humility,
> Raised by grace, faith, hope and charity.
> *Alleluia,* in order next following,
> Tokeneth prayer for our salvation,
> Twice remembered for laud and praising.

In the "Lay Folk's Mass Book" we are
thus instructed :

> . . . . Until that he the Gospel read ;
> Stand up then and take good heed,
> For then the priest flitteth his book
> North to that other altar nook ;
> And makes a cross upon the letter
> With his thumb, to speed him better,
> And then another on his face—
> For he hath mickle need of grace,
> For now an earthly man shall speak
> The words of Christ, God's Son so meek.
> Both the hearers and the preachers
> Have mickle need, methinks, of teachers,
> How they should read, and they should hear
> The words of God, so true and dear.

---

* i.e., degree, Latin *gradus*, a step, whence
Gradualis.

The Gospel

When the Epistle has been read by the
priest (or, at High Mass, chanted by the
subdeacon) on the south side of the altar,
and after the Gradual or other matter recited by the celebrant as above mentioned,
the latter proceeds to the north end of the
altar and there reads the Gospel from the
missal. If it be a High Mass, the deacon
then goes to that side of the chancel, carrying the book of the Gospels. This the subdeacon takes, and holds in front of himself,
with its back resting on his forehead. All
in the church then rise to their feet and
stand, out of reverence for the words of our
Lord. Two acolytes, with lighted torches
uplifted, take up a position one on each side
of the subdeacon, facing the deacon; and
with them goes the thurifer, holding the
smoking censer. The deacon takes the
censer and incenses the open Gospel, returns the censer to the thurifer, and then

standing with joined hands in front of the
book, sings: *Dominus vobiscum ;* to which the
choir respond: *Et cum spiritu tuo.* The
deacon then sings : *Initium (*or, *Sequentia)
sancti Evangelii secundum N.*—" Here be-
ginneth," or " continueth, the holy Gospel
according to St N."—and immediately makes
the sign of the cross, with his right thumb,
on the book, at the beginning of the passage
which he is about to read, and then on his
forehead, mouth and breast, in token that he
believes, professes and obeys the Gospel of
Jesus Christ. At the same time the choir
sing : *Gloria tibi Domine*—" Glory be to
Thee, O Lord "—while the deacon thrice incenses the book, for the Church pays to
the Gospels the highest marks of ecclesiastical honour. The congregation make
the triple sign of the cross, in the same
manner and at the same time as the deacon.
The chanting of the Gospel by the deacon
then proceeds in a Gregorian tone, which
varies only when the deacon is a member of
a religious order possessing a peculiar chant,
such as the Benedictines. As we have be-

ore observed, this ceremonial was anciently performed in the rood-loft.

It may be of interest to enquire why the Gospel is sung towards the north. This is at once explained when we remember that, according to immemorial tradition and usage, both Christian and Pagan, the north represents the *out*-side or, so to speak, the *wrong*-side of things. In pre-Christian mythology, the north, the quarter from whence come the storms and the cold, was regarded as the side of evil. In this way it came to be looked upon, in Christian times, as the devil's point of the compass, and as representing the outer darkness of heathendom. In that part of the churchyard which lay north of the church it was not usual to bury the bodies of any but excommunicated persons, pagans and the unbaptized. At a christening it was customary, when the priest came to the exorcism, to open wide the little door in the north wall of the baptistry or aisle, in order that the evil spirit of original sin might depart to his own place. When chanting the Gospel, the deacon faces north, because he is proclaiming the evangel primarily to the world of unbelief.

Concerning the use of lighted torches at the chanting of the Gospel, Dan Lydgate has these remarks :

> Afore the Gospel he needs must have fire,
> Torch, taper or wax candle light,
> In token that Christ (who consider aright)
> Is very brightness of light which is eterne,
> To chase away all darkness of the night,
> In perfect life to guiden us and govern.

It is curious to find the same idea reproduced in the Welsh "Ode to the Mass," composed by Ieuan ap Rhydderch in the fifteenth century :

> He needs must have fire when he sings it. . . .
> There must be fire skilfully made, beautiful.

Symbolically, the torches upheld at the Gospel typify Christ as *Lux Mundi*,—"the Light that enlighteneth every man that cometh into this world." Liturgically considered, the uplifted lights are a high form of ecclesiastical reverence, a mark of peculiar ritual honour paid to the words of our Lord.

We have somewhat minutely described
the ritual in connection with the reading of
the Gospel, because there is so much in
the way of folklore to notice under this
head.   Even now we have not exhausted
the subject ; but what remains must be
sought on a subsequent page, under the
heading " Last Gospel."

The Bidding Prayer

At the parochial Mass (i.e., the last and
High Mass sung on Sundays and great feasts
in the parish church, offered on the behalf
and for the benefit of the parishioners), the
parish priest or his curate ascends into the
pulpit and there makes any public announcements, preaches the sermon, or reads the
Bishop's Pastoral, as occasion may require.
Banns of intended marriage are first pro-
claimed ; then the names of sick members of
the congregation are given out, that prayer
may be said for their restoration to health ;
recent deaths and anniversaries are an-
nounced in order that God may be implored to give eternal rest to departed

souls; and the Epistle and the Gospel for
the day are read in the vulgar tongue. In
pre-Reformation times, before commencing
the sermon, the priest recited what was
known as the Bidding Prayer. This was a
form of supplication on behalf of all such
classes of persons as the congregation were
held bound in an especial manner to pray
for; and the order was usually the following, which I take from a document entitled "The Bedes* declared by Priests
in Church."

"Friends, you shall have on next Thurs-
day the feast of the Nativity of our blessed
Lord God, which day you shall keep as a
high and solemn feast ought to be kept; all
persons of sufficient age shall fast on
the eve.

"You shall now kneel down and make
your bedes to almighty God and our Lady
Saint Mary, and to all the holy company of
heaven, for the good estate and peace of our
holy mother the Church, that God maintain,
save and keep her.

* Bedes, or beads, means prayers.

"You shall pray for all Christian Catholic men and women, of what order, estate or degree soever they be, from the highest to the lowest.

"Firstly, for our holy father the Pope of Rome, with all his true college of cardinals; for all archbishops, bishops, abbots, priors, monks, canons, parsons, vicars and priests; and especially for the Archbishop of Canterbury, metropolitan and primate of England, and for my Lord of Wells, our diocesan.

"You shall pray also for the Holy Land and the Holy Sepulchre, that God may give it into the hands of Christian men, the more to be honoured for our prayers.

"You shall pray also for all them that have cure and charge of souls, as parsons, vicars and parish priests; that God give them grace so well to instruct their flocks that both curates and congregations, each in his degree, may so strive after healthful teaching that all may come to everlasting life.

"You shall pray also for all them that have taken any holy order, profession or re-

ligion upon them; and especially for my
Lord Abbot of Glastonbury, with all the
monastery, and for the vicar of this church,
and for all priests and clerks that serve in
this church; that God give them grace to
observe and keep their rule and persevere
in their holy duties, to the glory of God and
health of their souls.

"In the second place, you shall pray for
the unity and peace of all Christian realms,
and especially for the good estate, peace
and tranquillity of this realm of England;
for our sovereign Lord the King, the Queen,
the Prince of Wales, and for the peers and
commoners; that God give them grace so to
counsel, rule and govern, that it may be
honour to God, worship to themselves, and
profit unto the realm.

"You shall pray also for all women that
be in our Lady's bonds, * that God may
send the child right shape and christendom,
and to the mother purification of Holy
Church.

"You shall pray also for all true tillmen

---

* Pregnant of lawful progeny.

6

tithers, that God increase and multiply their store.

"You shall pray also for all manner fruits that be set or sown upon the earth; that God may send such seasonable weather as shall cause them to grow and increase plenteously, to the sustenance and help of all Christian folk.

"You shall pray also for all them that are sick or diseased in this parish or in any other, that God may send them health or turn them to the way that is most to His good pleasure and welfare of their souls.

"You shall pray also for all true pilgrims and palmers that have taken their way to Rome, Jerusalem, Compostella or any other holy place; that God give us participation in their good work, and to them participation in our prayers.

"You shall pray also for all them that find any light * in this church, or that give or have given any bequest as book, bell, chalice, vestment, altar-cloth or any other

---

* Maintain any lamp or taper burning before an altar, shrine, image or picture.

adornment whereby God's service hath been or is the better performed or upholden.

"You shall pray also for them that this day at holy Mass give bread to be hallowed;* for him that first began and them that longest continue this custom.

"In the third place, you shall pray, as you are bound, for the souls of your forefathers, parents, kindred, friends and benefactors, and for all those souls that are in the bitter pains of purgatory, there abiding the mercy of almighty God ; and especially for those souls that have most need and least help; as also for the souls of them whose bodies rest within the precincts of this church; that God grant unto them and to the souls of all the faithful departed eternal rest, light and peace.

"Every man and woman of you, of your charity say a *Pater*, *Ave* and *De Profundis*."

The Bidding Prayer, the above version of which is compiled from a collation of several copies, of different periods and dioceses, is so eminently Christian and Catholic that it

---

* Blessed bread ; see p. 109.

seems a pity it has fallen into disuse since the Reformation.

In a list of chantry lands at the Public Record Office,* dated 1548, is a reference to three acres of arable land in the parishes of Kenfig and Pile, Glamorgan, whereof one acre was given to find a light before the image of Mary Magdelyne in the church, and the other two "to be prayed for in the pulpit." This means that the lands were given to the Church in order that the donor's name might be added to the roll of bene-factors referred to in the Bidding Prayer.

Proceeding with his description of the Mass, the monk Lydgate says :

The Gospel read, a *Credo* after he saith,
  On solemn days, for a remembrance
Of twelve articles longing to our Faith,
  Which we are bound to have in our credence—
Rather to die, than any variance
  In any point were in our heart found.

*   *   *   *   *

As once Melchisedech, both priest and king,

---

* Chantries Certificate 74.   South Wales. 2 Ed. 6. (Printed in "Cardiff Records," Vol. II, p. 301.)

Gave bread and wine to Abraham for victory,
Which oblation, in figure remembering,
  Each day at Mass is said an Offertory,
Token that Jesus, our Saviour and our Lord,
  Against our feebleness, our impotence . . . .
In form of bread and wine, for a memory . . . .
Offered His Body, ground of our Offertory.

The Offertory

Leaving the pulpit, the priest returns to
the altar and resumes the celebration of Mass
by intoning the Nicene Creed: *Credo in unum
Deum*—"I believe in one God," etc. After
the Creed follow the prayers and ceremonies
connected with the offering of the bread and
wine, preliminary to their consecration. The
first of these prayers is one which varies according to the day, and is called the Offertory. At High Mass this is chanted by the
choir. It usually consists of a verse of a
psalm, preceded and followed by *Alleluia.*

It is at this stage of the Mass that the
faithful make their offerings. Nowadays this
is done simply by putting money into a plate
which is handed round among the congregation. In old times the offering was com-

monly made in the following manner : The
congregation rose from their places and filed
singly before the altar.   As each person
passed in front of the chancel gate, he placed
his offering in the hands of the deacon or
other minister appointed to receive it, who
stood within the gate, facing the people.
The offering consisted sometimes of money,
but most commonly of bread or wax candles
for the use of the sanctuary.   Sometimes
other things were offered, such as corn, oil,
wax, honey, eggs, butter and fruit.   At the
present day the clergy offer wax tapers at
their ordination ; and bishops at their consecration offer bread and wine.   At the
canonization of saints, bread, wine, water,
doves and other birds are offered. Pelliccia *
says that at the celebration of Mass " all
used to bring an offering of bread and wine,
first the men and then the women ; but all
offered the bread in white *fanons*, i.e., in
white linen cloths, that none might touch
with profane hands that bread which was to

* " Polity of the Christian Church " ; transl.
J. C. Bellett, M.A.   London, 1883 ; p. 237.

be consecrated." He adds that in the
Middle Ages the celebrant used to receive
the offerings, "going up to the altar rails,
where laymen were allowed to present them ;
while presbyters, the clergy and the Emperor,
used to bring their offerings to the altar itself, within the rails." The gifts were placed
upon the credence table and there remained
during the Mass.

In England also it was the custom for the
congregation to go up to present their offerings in some rough order of precedence ; the
squire first, followed by any other gentleman
of the parish ; these by the yeomen, merchants and artisans, and they in turn by
peasants and labourers. The women followed
in like order. It is not surprising that squab-
bles as to precedence often arose, especially
among ladies. Some of these disputes remain on record in the ancient archives of our
courts of law.

Among the offerings made at High Mass
on Sundays were loaves for the hallowed
bread, which will be referred to on a later
page. Special offerings, in money or kind,

were made at the first Mass said or sung by
a newly ordained priest.

"To offer," as our Catholic ancestors expressed it, was considered by them a necessary incident to devout attendance at Mass;
and few were so poor as not to take their
"offering-penny" or "Mass-penny" to the
chancel steps.

A curious question presents itself in connection with the manual acts performed by
the celebrant at the altar, namely, why he
blesses the water which he is about to mix
with the wine in the chalice, but not the
wine itself? The *Ritus Celebrandi Missam*
has these directions: "Then, standing at
the Epistle side, he takes the chalice, dries
it with the purificatory, and, holding it (the
chalice) by the knot, takes the phial of wine
from the hand of the minister . . . . and
puts wine into the chalice. Then, in the
same manner holding the chalice, he makes
the sign of the cross upon the phial of water,
and says (the prayer) *Deus qui humanæ sub-
stantiæ*, and pouring a little water into the
chalice, continues," etc. This infusing of
water into the wine is well known to be

symbolical of the two natures of Christ,
and of the water and blood which flowed
from the Saviour's side at the Crucifixion;
but we must leave it to skilled liturgists to
explain why, in the case above cited, the
water is blessed but not the wine.

The simple and almost supernatural
beauty of the chant known as the Preface,
sung partly in versicle and response between
priest and choir, and partly by the priest
alone, is well known to every one, Catholic
or non-Catholic, who has ever been present
at a sung Mass. Gounod is said to have
declared that he would rather have the
honour of having composed the music of
the Preface than any music made by himself or any other composer.

The Ter Sanctus

The Preface terminates in the *Sanctus*
("Holy holy, holy," etc.). On the priest's
pronouncing this triple adjuration of almighty God, the little bell on the altar step
is rung thrice by the clerk or an acolyte.
At the same time a bell outside the church
used to be triply tolled. This bell (now

sounded at the Elevation) hangs in a turret
on the roof, just over the chancel arch, and
is rung by means of a cord which hangs
down through the roof into the chancel.
Here the end of the cord is grasped by an
acolyte who kneels just inside the altar rails,
on the Epistle side. This bell is called the
"Sanctus bell" or, in mediæval English, the
"Saunts bell." The little bell ring at the
foot of the altar is termed a "sacring bell,"
sacring being the old word for consecration.

Next the Secret after the Offertory,
The Preface followeth, afore the Sacrament.
Angels rejoice with laud, honour and glory.
From the heavenly court by grace they are sent.
And at the Mass abide and are present,
All our prayers devoutly to report
To Him that sits above the firmament.
Souls in peyne they refresh and comfort.
The old prophet, holy Isaie,
Saw high in heaven a throne of dignity,
Where Seraphs sang, with every hierarchy,
Sanctus, sanctus, afore the Trinity,
After the Preface, rehersed times three
With voice melodious, and after the *Osanna*
High *in excelsis*, before the Majesty.

The Beginning of the Canon

Immediately upon the *Sanctus* there follows a prayer beginning with the words *Te igitur* ("Thee, therefore, most clement Father," etc.) This begins the practically unchanged and unchangeable central portion of the Mass.

In the Hereford Missal, the local redaction of the Roman Missal, as anciently used in the diocese of Hereford and in parts of South Wales, the initial letter T of the first word in the *Te igitur* was always written very large, and beautifully illuminated in gold and colours, with a miniature of our Lord in the rounded body of the Gothic T. Before commencing the *Te igitur*, the priest used to kiss this little picture and say the prayer *Adoremus te Christe.** In altar-missals of the present day, an engraving of the Crucifixion occupies the left-hand page, facing the *Te igitur*.

* "We adore Thee, O Christ, because by Thy Cross Thou hast redeemed the world."

The Elevation

We will now suppose that the solemn words of consecration have been softly, slowly and distinctly pronounced over the Host by the celebrant of the Mass, and that to the eye of faith, instead of a white flour wafer and a little pure grape wine, the Divine presence is really and substantially with this congregation of the faithful.

Immediately after uttering the words of consecration, the priest genuflects in adoration, and then, for a moment, elevates the Host a little higher than his head, without turning towards the people. The sacring-bell at the same time rings thrice and is answered by three deep tones from the tower or sanctus-bell turret. The like ensues upon the consecration of the contents of the chalice, which is similarly elevated. The tolling of the sanctus-bell is to give notice to absent parishioners that the Consecration has taken place, and to enable them to perform a brief act of homage to our Lord present in the blessed Sacrament.   Catholics who hear the sound, wherever they may be, make the sign of the cross and say a short mental prayer.

As is natural, much of the folklore of the Mass has reference to the Elevation.   The object of the uplifting of the Host and chalice is to present the blessed Sacrament for the adoration of the people.   In the Middle Ages the faithful were accustomed to look at the uplifted Host and chalice before bending in prayer, and there is abundant evidence that importance was attached to this observance—so much so, indeed, that attendance at Mass was often spoken of as "seeing God."   The best known mediæval manual of devotions at Mass—*The Lay Folk's Mass Book*, says :

> When time is nigh of sacring,
> A little bell they use to ring ;
> Then is reason that we do reverence
> To Jesu Christ His presence,
> That comes to loose all baleful bands.
> Therefore, kneeling, hold up thy hands,
> And with inclination of thy body
> Behold the Levation reverently.

A Welsh bard, Morys ap Hywel, about the year 1530 composed a certain ode which begins: "Let us go over yonder to the church in three hosts, on Sunday to see Jesus."* The allusion is certainly to the Elevation at Mass.

Dan Lydgate, in his "Vertue of the Masse," thus counsels his readers, in his Renascence style:

First every morrow, or Phœbus shine bright,
Let pale Aurora conduct you and dress
To holy church, of Christ to have a sight,
For chief preservative against all ghostly sickness.

We have already noticed similar phraseology in the ancient Welsh treatise entitled "The merits (or virtues) of seeing the Body of Christ." So, also, another version of the *Lay Folk's Mass Book*:

Therefore, with fear and pure intent
Thou must behold this Sacrament.

Googe, in his *Popish Kingdome*, seems

---

* Awn draw i'r llan yn dri llu
Dydd Sul i weled Iesu.
                    —(MS., Cardiff Free Library.)

to refer to this idea when, writing satirically
of the sacring bell, he says :

Yea, if the bell to sacring toll, and far from thence
    thou be
And cannot come, but earnestly do wish the same
    to see,
A merit great you gotten have. . . .

It will be remembered that Queen
Elizabeth manifested her Protestant sym-
pathies at the very beginning of her reign by
forbidding the celebrant of the Mass, which
she attended in state, to elevate the Host.
" The queen," says Dr Lee,* " being present
at the Bishop of Carlisle's Mass, soon after
her accession—on Christmas morning, as
some assert, and while the cantors of her
chapel were singing the *Gloria in excelsis* at
their lectern—sent a message to his lordship
within the sanctuary peremptorily forbidding
him to elevate the Host.   But Oglethorpe
replied that, as it was the unvarying rule of
the Catholic Church for all priests to do so,
he must ask Her Majesty's permission to

* *The Church under Queen Elizabeth,* by F.
G. Lee. London, 1880 ; vol. i, p. 12.

allow him to conform.   Upon this, before
the Gospel . . . . she rose from her fald-
stool, biting her thin lips in anger . . . .
stamped vigorously on the floor, and so
hastily departed."   A few days later Elizabeth succeeded in preventing the Elevation ;
and thus significantly and appropriately in-
augurated the establishment of the royal
supremacy in matters spiritual, and the dis-
continuance of public Catholic worship, by
an act of hostility to the blessed Sacrament.

This was the period of blasphemous re-
volt on the part of a small but violent section
of the English people, when the Consecration
was denounced as juggling, and its words
parodied as *hocus pocus ;* when, at the Elevation, a Protestant once in derision held
aloft a dog, and the blessed Sacrament was
contemptuously and impiously referred to
under the terms "Jack-in-the-box" and
" Round Robin "—words which are nowadays used with no suspicion of their original
significance.

Googe, writing of the processions of Corpus Christi, has these lines :

The people flat on faces fall, their hands held up
    on high,
Believing that they see their God and sovereign
    Majesty ;
The like at Mass they do, while as the bread is
    lifted well
And chalice shewed aloft, when as the sexton
    rings the bell.

The following lines are taken from Lydgate's prayer to be said at the Elevation of the Host :

Hail, holy Jesu, our health, our ghostly Food ;
    Hail, blessed Lord, here in form of Bread ;
Hail, for mankind offered on the rood
    For our redemption, with Thy Blood made red,
    Stung to the Heart with a spear's head.
Now, gracious Jesu, for Thy Woundes five,
    Grant of Thy mercy, before that I be dead,
Clean shrift and housel while I am here alive.

     *   *   *   *   *

O blessed Fruit, born of a pure Virgin,
    Who with Thy Passion boughtest me so dear,
For Mary's sake Thine ears down incline,
    Hear mine orison by mean of her prayer ;
    Thee for to please teach me the manere.

Void of all virtue save only of Thy grace,
Grant in the form that I see Thee here,
  Thee to receive I may have life and space.
My Lord, my Maker, my Saviour and my King,
  When I was lost, Thou wert my Redemptor,
Support and succour here in this living,
  Against all enemies my sovereign Protector,
  My chief comfort in all worldly labour.

     *   *   *   *   *

Let Thy Mother be present in this need,
  That I may claim, of mercy more than of right,
Mine heritage, for which Thou didest bleed.
  And grant me, Jesu, of Thy gracious might,
  Each day of Thee for to have a sight,
For ghostly gladness, to my life's end ;
  And in spirit, to make my heart light,
Thee to receive ere I hence wend.

     *   *   *   *

Grant ere I die, Christ, for Thy Passion,
I may receive this Bread sent down from heaven.

So closely was the Mass associated with the family life of our ancestors, that even heraldry bears witness of the fact. To say nothing of the *Agnus Dei* or Paschal Lamb, which, as the "Lamb and the Flag," still figures on some inn-signs, the Host has come down to us in the form of a heraldic charge in the armorial bearings of a few ancient families—as, for instance, on the shield of the Scottish house, Tyrie of Lunan, who bear : Sable, a chevron between three plates each charged with a cross between the capital letters I and S, also sable.   In non-heraldic language these charges are three Mass-wafers bearing the sacred monogram.

An old remedy for the whooping-cough was to drink wine out of the chalice, the draught to be administered by a priest. This belief survived in the hill-country of South Wales to a recent date ; and it is curious to note that the Calvinists would not think of applying to any minister of religion but a Catholic priest to administer the antidote.

In *Notes and Queries* for July 19, 1902, is a communication by A. H. Baverstock, under the heading " Merry England and the Mass," to the following effect :

" A passage in Becon—I have not the reference—seems to indicate a prevailing idea in England that the sight of the Host at the elevation brought joy to the heart. Becon describes how at this moment in the service a man would jostle his neighbour in his eagerness to look on the Holy Sacrament, exclaiming that he ' could not be blithe until he had seen his Lord God that day,' or words to that effect."

Another work of Lydgate's, a set of verses entitled " How the Good Wife taught her Daughter," * has these lines :

> Look lovely and in good life,
> Thou love God and Holy Church,
> Go to church when thou may—
> Look thou spare for no rain—
> For thou farest the best that ilke day
> When thou has God y-seen.

Regarding the *Memento* of the Dead, which follows soon after the Consecration, Lydgate observes :

> Of *Memento* at Mass there be twain :
> The first remembreth of folks that be alive;
> And the second for them that suffer peyne. . . .
> Singing of Masses, and Christ's Passion,
> And remembrance of His Wounds five,
> May best avail to their remission.

---

* MS. *circa* 1430, printed by the Early English Text Society.

The Pater Noster

This greatest of all prayers, the only one directly taught by God, finds a fitting place in the greatest of all sacrifices, itself of divine institution.

The various prayers which compose the Canon of the Mass are linked together in one chain of impetration.   Thus the ancient and beautiful chant of the *Pater Noster* commences with the words *Per omnia sæcula sæculorum, amen*, which are the conclusion of the preceding prayer.   Then, joining his hands, the priest says or chants in Latin: "Let us pray.   Instructed by Thy saving precepts, and following Thy divine directions, we presume to say : Our Father," etc.   The prayer itself is said by the priest with hands extended.   The concluding petition, *Sed libera nos a malo*, is not said by him but by the clerk, or deacon, and sung by the choir, the priest responding in a low voice, *Amen*—thus reversing the usual order of versicle and re

sponse.   The *Pater noster* is thereupon con-
tinued or paraphrased by the priest in the
further prayer, *Libera nos quæsumus*, in which
he beseeches almighty God to deliver us from
all evils, past, present and future, and to grant
us, by the intercession of all saints, freedom
from sin and security from all trouble,
through Jesus Christ.   It is while concluding
this prayer that the celebrant performs the
important liturgical and sacrificial act of the
fraction or breaking of the Host over the
chalice.

A curious question arises in regard to
this prayer *Libera nos quæsumus*.   The saints
whose intercession is here especially referred
to are " the ever blessed and glorious Virgin
Mary, Mother of God, with Thy blessed
Apostles Peter and Paul and Andrew and
all saints " ; for whose sake almighty God is
implored to " graciously give peace in our
days."   I have never met with an explanation
of the inclusion of St Andrew's name in this
place; Canon Oakley, in his admirable little
book on the *Ceremonies of the Mass*, does
not refer to the point, yet it would seem

to call for elucidation. We might have
expected the name of St John Baptist,
than whom no greater was born of woman;
or of St John Evangelist, the beloved dis-
ciple; but the saint who is thus brought
into such close association with our Lady,
with the Prince of the Apostles, and with the
great Doctor of the Nations, is just the
humble fisherman who was crucified at
Patræ. It can hardly be supposed that
St Andrew is thus distinguished because he
was St Peter's brother in the flesh, and one
would like to see the solution of this
problem.

In the ancient Celtic Church such extreme importance was attached to a correct
recitation of the *Pater Noster* in the Mass,
that long and severe penances were enjoined
for the smallest slip in pronouncing any
word of this prayer. The priest who mis-
pronounced any part of the *Pater Noster*
had to undergo many days of rigorous
fasting and severe scourgings. Little wonder, therefore, that the Celtic monks referred to the Lord's Prayer as *Oratio quæ*

dicitur periculosa—" The prayer which is called perilous." That the prayer taught by our merciful Lord should be thus designated, is a curious illustration of the exaggerated asceticism to which the perfervid Celtic genius lent itself in those early ages.

The *Pater Noster* of the days before St Jerome's translation of the Bible followed the version of the Scriptures known as the *Vetus Itala*, or old Italic, and the fourth petition ran : *Panem nostrum supersubstantialem da nobis hodie*—" Give us this day our supersubstantial Bread "—a phrase which bore direct reference to the Blessed Eucharist.*

Ancient Welsh scrap-book MSS. often comprise a tract entitled " A Treatise on the Seven Prayers of the Pater," † meaning

---

* In the Middle Ages the article of the Creed as to the "communion of saints "—*sanctorum communionem*—was often interpreted to mean "communion of the holy things," i.e., of the blessed Sacrament.

† Traethawd ar Saith Weddi y Pader.

thereby the seven petitions of the Pater-noster.

The Pax

The extension of the *Pater Noster* con-cludes with *Per omnia sæcula sæculorum, amen;* whereupon the priest, making the sign of the cross thrice over the chalice with a particle of the Host, says: *Pax Domini sit semper vobiscum*—" The peace of our Lord be always with you," to which the deacon or clerk, or the choir, responds "And with thy spirit." It is the custom in Catholic countries to make the sign of the cross upon one's forehead, mouth and breast as the priest pronounces this blessing, which, historically considered, is the most ancient benediction in the Liturgy.

Dipping the particle of the Host into the chalice, the celebrant next prays: " May this mingling and consecration of the Body and Blood of our Lord Jesus Christ be unto us who receive them life eternal. Amen." Then, after a genuflection, he says, striking his breast thrice, the threefold *Agnus Dei;*

" Lamb of God, who takest away the sins of the world, have mercy on us," "Give us peace," or, in Masses of requiem, " Give to them eternal rest." Next, with hands joined upon the altar, and body bending forward, he says the beautiful prayer: "O Lord Jesus Christ, who saidst to Thy Apostles, 'Peace I leave to you, My peace I give unto you,'" etc., for the peace of Christ's Church. If it be a High Mass, the celebrant now kisses the altar, and turning to the right, gives the ecclesiastical *accolade* to the deacon, by placing his hand upon the deacon's shoulder, saying at the same time *Pax tecum*—" Peace be with thee "; to which the response is *Et cum spiritu tuo*—" And with thy spirit." The celebrant then proceeds with the prayers which precede the Communion; but the deacon gives a like embrace to the subdeacon, and he in turn to the next minister in order of dignity. This ceremony is called "giving the *Pax*."

A custom which is but rarely witnessed in this country at the present day, even at the most solemn celebration of High Mass, is the ceremony of giving the *Pax* to the congregation through the medium of an object called in Latin *osculatorium*—in English a pax-board. After the celebrant has passed on the fraternal embrace to the other officiating clergy, as above described, he kisses the pax-board ; which an acolyte thereupon carries around to be kissed successively by the male members of the congregation, or at least by those in the vicinity of the chancel. The pax-board is a tablet of gold, silver or ivory, having carved on the front of it some representation of our Lord (usually the Paschal Lamb), and at the back a handle. The great national museums contain examples of *osculatoria* which are exquisite works of art. In very ancient times it was often the book of the Gospels or a small crucifix which was so kissed.

The reformer Tyndale in 1528 wrote : "To kisse the paxe they thinke a meritorious deed."*

"The Vertue of the Masse" has the

* *Obedience of a Christian Man.* London, 1572, p. 154.

following passages anent the *Agnus Dei* and
the *Pax* :

> Of *Agnus Dei* at Mass be said three :
> The first two beseeching of mercy ;
> The third prayeth for peace and unity
> Against all peril mortal and worldly,
> Against troubles dreadful and fleshly.
> Christ as a Lamb was offered on the cross ;
> Grudged not, suffered patiently,
> To make redemption and reform our loss.
>
> *   *   *   *   *   *
>
> This *Agnus Dei* brought with Him peace
> To all the world, at His Nativity,
> Grace, gladness, of virtue great increase ;
> For which the people, of high and low
>   degree,
> Kiss the pax—a token of unity.

The Communion

The folklore of this part of the Mass has
reference less to Holy Communion itself
than to devotional practices which are
associated with it more or less closely.
There is, however, some interesting lan-
guage-lore attached to this subject. The
old English term for Holy Communion
was "housel," an Anglo-Saxon word. "To

housel " was to administer the Holy Communion. " Houselling-bread " meant the
wafers for consecration (which were also
termed " singing-breads.") The " houselling-
cloth " was the linen cloth laid over the altar-
rails to be held by the " houselling-folk "
or communicants ; while the " houselling-
bell " was that which rang at the *Domine
non sum dignus*. The familiar phrase of
Shakespeare, to die " unhouselled, disap-
pointed, unannealed," meant without holy
Viaticum, absolution or extreme unction,
respectively—though the rhythm interfered
with the proper sequence, which requires
absolution to precede the houselling.

Intimately connected with the Holy
Communion, though quite distinct there-
from, was the hallowing and distribution of
" blessed bread," a very ancient practice
which first arose out of the offering (or,
perhaps, out of the love-feasts of the primitive Church), but which has not been used
in this country since the Reformation.
When leavened bread was offered, a portion was kept to be bestowed on the poor,

and the rest was placed upon the credence-
table by the subdeacon.   Here it was
blessed by the celebrant, cut up into small
pieces and distributed to the congregation.
Those who have attended High Mass at a
French cathedral or parish church will remember that at the Offertory or immediately
after the Communion, acolytes carry round
to the people holy bread on large salvers or
in baskets, each person taking a piece and
eating it, though sometimes he takes it
home.   Many people on receiving blessed
bread, say:

> Pain béni, je te prends ;
> Si la mort me surprend,
> Sers-moi de saint-Sacrement.

That is: " Blessed bread, I take thee ; if
death overtake me, be thou to me as the
Holy Sacrament."   In England and Wales,
in ancient times, the faithful were instructed
not to regard the blessed bread as in any
way an effective substitute for Holy Communion.   They were taught the same also
with respect to the practice, usual in those
days, of communicants drinking wine from a

chalice after Communion. Both these usages had their origin in a profound veneration for the Holy Eucharist, and doubtless the reason why they were not retained throughout the Western Church was that they were liable to be misconstrued by simple and unlettered folk.

The same may be said as to the mediæval symbolic Communion, a beautiful and poetic custom of chivalry. On the eve of battle, when neither Eucharist nor priest was to be had, the knights would administer to each other, as a symbol of the Blessed Sacrament, three blades of grass, in token of the Holy Trinity, after making their confessions òne to another in private.

Mediæval literature abounds in allusions to the hallowed bread ; and we have already cited examples from old Welsh manuscripts, as, for instance, the bardic assurance that happiness should be the lot of him who heard Mass and took blessed bread after. (See *ante*, p. 21.)

In 1549 the Catholic insurgents of Devon and Cornwall, who made so valiant a struggle for the restoration of the Mass, insisted, among other points, that they would have "blessed bread and holy water made every Sunday . . . . and all other ancient old ceremonies used heretofore by our Mother the holy Church." *

Before leaving this branch of our subject, it may be of interest to remark that in some cathedrals and large monastic and parish churches, before the Reformation, the "singing-breads" or Mass-wafers were made in the sacred building itself. This is attested by the ovens and the wafer-tongs which still remain in some churches; and also by the directions, to be found in mediæval manuscripts, for the decent and proper preparation of the wafers by sextons, nuns or lay-brethren.

This is a convenient point at which to pay some attention to the subject of the saints of the Canon, i.e., the saints who are commemorated by name in this portion of the Mass. These are, besides the Blessed

* Dr Lee, *Edward VI, Supreme Head;* second edition, p. 127.

Virgin and the Apostles, Saints Linus, Cletus, Clement, Xystus, Cornelius, Cyprian, Laurence, Chrysogonus, John and Paul, Cosmas and Damian (all named before the Consecration), and Ignatius, Alexander, Marcellinus, Peter, Felicitas, Perpetua, Agatha, Lucy, Agnes, Cecily and Anastasia—the last eleven being mentioned after the Consecration.   It is of interest to note that this list contains the names of those Romans who had suffered martyrdom prior to the "closing" or final settlement of the Canon.   It will be noticed that the last seven are women.   These saints were commemorated in the Mass of the Church of the catacombs, celebrated, in some cases, on the very tombs of those who had witnessed with their blood to the Faith of Christ.

The Conclusion of Mass

After the priest had taken Holy Communion in both kinds, and had rinsed the chalice and performed the ablutions, he formerly poured the water of the final ablution into the piscina.   This, which is a shallow,

grooved basin carved in a niche of the south
wall of the chancel, has a drain or conduit
from the bowl to the earth below the chancel
floor.   The piscina is so constructed in order
to carry the water of the ablutions directly into
the soil, thus avoiding all danger of profana-
tion to any particles which might remain of
the Blessed Sacrament.   The piscina may
still be seen in many old parish churches,
especially in such as have been conserva-
tively restored by a competent architect with
ecclesiological knowledge.   In unrestored
churches the piscina remains hidden behind
the plaster with which it was covered at the
Reformation, when the abolition of the Mass
rendered it superfluous.

The ablutions having been performed,
the priest reads the passage called the Communion, and the prayer known as the Postcommunion ; and then, at the middle of the
altar, turns to the congregation and says or
intones, *Ite, missa est*—" Go, Mass is over,"
or *Benedicamus Domino*—" Let us bless the
Lord"—according to the day ; the response to
either being *Deo gratias*—" Thanks be to

God." Turning to the people again, he im-
parts to the kneeling congregation the priestly
blessing : *Benedicat vos omnipotens Deus,
Pater et Filius et Spiritus Sanctus, amen—*
"The blessing of Almighty God, Father, Son
and Holy Ghost, be upon you, amen."

The Last Gospel

Passing to the north end of the altar,
the priest now reads the Last Gospel—
usually the beginning of the Gospel according to St John—in an undertone, whether
the Mass be High or Low. The congregation stand and bless themselves as at the
Gospel of the Mass.

Too often Catholics are wont to attach
but slight importance to the Last Gospel. If
we are in a hurry we perhaps leave the
church as soon as the celebrant has given his
blessing ; and we sometimes wonder why the
reading of a Latin Gospel is tacked on to the
end of the Mass. Previous to the sixteenth
century the priest usually recited it from memory on his way back to the sacristy ; but at
a much earlier period it had become the

occasional custom for a Gospel to be read by
the celebrant before leaving the altar. People
would give the priest an offering to read a
Gospel of their own choosing, for the good
estate of the offerer or for the repose of the
souls of his deceased friends.   At one time
this was done to such an extent that a priest
might have to read several Gospels, whereby
divine service was greatly protracted.   This
inconvenience led to the settling of the
rubric on this point as it stands at present, in
conformity with the Missal of Pope Pius V.

A custom prevailed among all Christians,
in very early times, of carrying on the person
a copy of the Gospels, or of one Gospel, or of
some portion of a Gospel, as a supernatural protection against evil.   This practice may pos-
sibly have originated in a desire to have an
opportunity of studying the sacred Scriptures
at any leisure moment; but it seems to have
soon degenerated into a tendency to use the
Gospels as something in the nature of a
charm or amulet—a typical instance of the
way in which the holiest things are liable to
be degraded by an unworthy use of them.

The portion of the Gospels which was most commonly worn on the person for these purposes was the first fourteen verses of the first chapter of St John's Gospel : *In principio erat Verbum*—" In the beginning was the Word," etc.   The reason of this was doubtless its beautiful and mystic allusions to light and life, and the occurrence of the sacrosanct confession of the faith : *Et Verbum caro factum est, et habitavit in nobis*—" And the Word was made flesh, and dwelt among us," which is the doctrinal foundation-stone of Christianity.

Tyndale, the reformer, did not forget to make capital out of these extravagances of popular devotion.   Describing the custom of his time in what is probably exaggerated language, he writes : * "Thousandes, while the priest pattereth S. John's Gospell in Latine ouer their heades, crosse themselues with, I trow a legion of crosses, behynde and before, and . . . . plucke vp their legges and crosse so much as their heeles and the very soles of their fete, and beleue that if it

* *Obedience of a Christian Man.*

be done in the time that he readeth the
gospel . . . . that there shal no mischaunce
happen them that day." In another passage*
he says sarcastically: "If any be sicke, go also
and say over them a Gospell and all in Latin."

He refers also † to "St Agathe's letter
written in the Gospell tyme, and . . . . yᵉ
crosses on palme-sonday made in the passion
tyme‡ . . . . the saying of gospels vnto
women in childbed.   Such is the . . . .
saying of *in principio erat verbum* from house
to house.   Such is the saying of gospels to
the corne in the field in the procession §
weeke that it should the better grow."

The one pre-Reformation popular devotion which survives in the memory of the
English rural classes in every county is an
invocation of the four Evangelists which
was recited by children on going to bed :

Matthew, Mark, Luke and John,
Bless the bed that I lie on.

---

* Ib., p. 135.   † Ib. p. 271.
‡ i.e., during the reading of the Gospels of
the Passion.
§ Rogation.

> Four corners to my bed,
> Four angels round my head ;
> Two to guard me as I lie,
> And two to take me when I die.

The change of religion has had the effect
of attaching an almost comical sense to the
above rhyme, at all events in the minds of
Protestants.   For my own part, the verses
strike me as simple, dignified and Christian.
They are certainly very ancient, and quite
worthy of preservation.

Allusion has already been made to the
ancient procession to the high altar for
solemn Mass.   It was carried out with great
pomp, especially when the bishop pontifi-
cated ; and the Gospels were its principal
object.   The officiating clergy and ministers
clad in their sacred vestments, and with
lights, incense and holy water, wended their
way up the nave of the church, chanting a
litany.   The deacon carried the splendidly
bound and illuminated Gospel-book, the
cover of which would in those days be of
some precious metal, carved with a representation of the Crucifixion, and the sym-

bols of the four evangelists, and studded with gems.   The external reverence paid to the book of the Gospels in old times was very great.   Often it was brought by the deacon to the chancel steps, where every member of the congregation knelt and kissed the cross on its cover, as is still done in some oriental rites.

Oaths were solemnly taken " on the holy Gospels of God," and this phrase was retained in some legal documents down to the nineteenth century.   Special honour was paid, as we have seen, to the commencement of St John's Gospel.   The initial letter of its opening verse was always written, or rather, drawn, very large, and was ornamented with the utmost skill of the limner, in brilliant gold and the richest colours.

From all that has been said on this point, it may be seen how the Catholic Church has always honoured and reverenced the holy Gospel of our redemption, paying to it the highest worship (in the original and orthodox sense of that word) which she accords to any material object, and which the Gospel-book shares only with altars, the relics of saints, the holy oils, the paschal candle, the cross on Good Friday, and the person of the bishop—we allude to the ecclesiastical honour expressed by the acts of incensing, sprinkling with holy water, kissing and genuflection.

Dan Lydgate lays great stress on the importance of remaining in church after Mass until the priest has finished reading the last Gospel:

> Ent'ring the church with all humility
>   To hear Mass, on morrow at your rising,
> Dispose yourself, kneeling on your knee,
>   For to be there, first at the beginning.
>   From the time of his revesting,
> Depart you not till the time he hath doo;
>   To all your works it shall be great furthering
> To abide the end of *In principio*.
>
>   *   *   *   *   *   *
>
> A work begun is of more avail
>   If a good end accord well thereto;
> And, for increase of your ghostly travail,
>   Abide at Mass till *In principio*.

VI—The Attitude of Prayer

It may be permitted to say something with
regard to the external attitude of prayer at
Mass.   The primitive rule was that Christians should pray standing on Sundays, but
on other days kneeling.   Even at the present
time it is strictly correct to stand at High
Mass whenever the celebrant is chanting.
It is to be regretted that we in this country
do not pay greater attention to the proprieties in this respect.   There can be no doubt
that the men in the congregation should
stand when the priest is proceeding towards
the altar, especially for High Mass, though
if a bishop be in the procession, it is right
to kneel for his blessing as he passes.   In
England and Wales the congregation are
accustomed to sit down after the *Et homo
factus est*, and to remain seated during the
offertory and until the bell rings at the
Sanctus.   To kneel at the *Sanctus* is, no
doubt, very proper (though it is not the

general custom abroad) ; but to sit at the
offertory is not a laudable practice, and per-
plexes Catholics of other nationalities.

The early Christians prayed with arms
uplifted from the elbow, and hands extended with the palms to the front. This is
the attitude in which are depicted the
oranti of the catacombs; and it is still
retained by Catholics of various nationalities, such as the Irish and the Maltese
—more especially by the aged and in
presence of the Blessed Sacrament.

A priest, or an acolyte taking part in
the Liturgy as minister, has his hands together, with fingers joined at the tips, and
his elbows close to his side. This is, perhaps, also the most becoming posture for
a layman to adopt at prayer, especially
during Mass, if he is not using a book.
He must, of course, be careful to avoid
anything like attitudinising ; but few Catholics are likely to err in that direction.

Since the eighteenth century, Catholics
seem to have acquired a habit of semi-
prostration during the Consecration and

Elevation, and at the moment of Benediction.   The ancient practice was to look at
the Sacred Host, and to bow the head in
adoration only at the moment when the
priest genuflected—i.e., between the second
and third ringing of the sacring-bell.   This
would seem to be the most correct practice.

To strike the bréast thrice at the *Domine
non sum dignus* is a pious and eminently
Catholic practice of immemorial antiquity,
though too often neglected by Catholics of
the younger generation.

It is a pity that some Catholics nowadays
omit to make the triple sign of the cross at the
commencement of the reading of the Gospel ;
as also to bow at the words, *Adoramus te,
gratias agimus tibi, Jesu Christe,* in the "Gloria
in excelsis," etc.   In these days of florid
music, the link between the priest and ministers in the chancel and the congregation in
the church is all too slight.   The observance
of the liturgical proprieties above referred to
is useful as tending to strengthen and maintain it, and as reminding the layfolk that they
are *assisting* at the Mass—not mere spectators.

The poor " Mass-houses," which the piety of the faithful erected in this country on the first relaxation of the Penal Laws at the end of the eighteenth century, contained but one altar. Hence arose the custom, almost peculiar to the British Isles, of reserving the Blessed Sacrament upon the high altar instead of in a side chapel, and the consequent confusion in the practice of bowing and genuflection.

Genuflection is made not to the altar, but to the Blessed Sacrament. In passing an altar at which the Most Holy is not reserved, a Catholic bows to the crucifix, but does not genuflect.

On passing or approaching an altar whereon the Blessed Sacrament is exposed— either in a monstrance or pyx, or because Mass is there being said and the Host has been consecrated and not yet consumed— the Catholic adores our Lord by kneeling for a moment on both knees and bowing the head.

On Good Friday genuflection should be made to the crucifix. On Holy Saturday and at other times when the altar is bare and the tabernacle empty and open because Jesus is not there, we bow to the figure of the Crucified, but do not genuflect.

Probably very few of us neglect to take holy water on entering the church for Mass, and one cannot be too careful to observe this ancient and pious custom. Besides acquiring the benefit of the prayers and blessings with which the Church has consecrated " this creature of water," the devout Catholic thereby testifies his desire to purify his heart and mind for the due perception of the Sacred Mysteries instituted by the God of all purity. Ritual lustration was one of the intrinsically innocent practices which the primitive Church took over from pre-Christian religion and adapted to the service of the Christ. The blessing of water for ritual and pious uses has been the Church's custom through all the ages, and particularly in connection with Sunday Mass. Water is blessed only on Sunday, for the *Asperges* which precedes the parochial Mass of that day, and for placing in the stoup which is fixed by the principal door of every Catholic church.

A Hymn at the Elevation of· the Host *

(MS. of the year 1456. Spelling and punctuation modernized.)

Whosoever says this prayer between the Levation and the three " Agnus," shall have the pardon granted by Pope Boniface VI.

Welcome, Lord, in form of bread ;
In Thee is both life and death,
  Jesus is Thy Name.
Thou art God in Trinity ;
Lord, have mercy now on me,
  Shield Thou me from shame.

Hail Father, hail Son,
Hail Holy Ghost from heaven come ;
  Heaven's King art Thou.
Hail Man of might most,
Father, Son and Holy Ghost,
  Of Mary Thou wert born.

Hail Jesus, blessed Thou be,
Hail Blossom on the tree,
  Blessed be Thou Son.
Hail Fruit, hail Flower,
Hail Jesus our Saviour,
  On water and on land.

---

* MS. Harl. 5,396, 38 h. No. 3.

Hail King, Cæsar and Knight,
Hail Man most of might,
  Prince on Thy throne.
Hail Duke, hail Emperour,
Hail be Thou most of honour
  Of all this world.

Hail Flesh, hail Blood,
Hail Man of mild mood,
  Hail heaven's King.
Hail be Thou, Baron best,
Hail Father fairest,
  Thou madest all thing.

Hail Rose upon ryse,
Hail peerless of price,
  For us Thou wert dead.
Hail Jesu that all things wost,
Hail Father, Son and Holy Ghost ;
  Welcome, Lord, in form of bread.

* Branch.

www.ingramcontent.com/pod-product-compliance
Lightning Source LLC
La Vergne TN
LVHW090046090426
835511LV00031B/326